"Roger Martin understands how we got to where we are in the United States today. He is not happy but refuses to give up, offering proposals to restore life in our political system, which is too far divided economically. His proposals won't be easy to enact, but they need urgent attention if we are to save the best chance for democratic capitalism. A must-read!"

—The late Paul Volcker, former Chairman, US Federal Reserve

"In *When More Is Not Better*, Roger Martin leverages his deep knowledge of economic systems to precisely diagnose the systemic shortcomings of the modern economy and his practical experience to lay out a pathway to an economy that works for all. A must-read."

—Paul Polman, cofounder and Chair, IMAGINE; former CEO, Unilever

"Friction and separation are good; efficiency and connectedness are overrated. These are some of the important, if surprising, messages in this book by one of the world's most creative business minds. Roger Martin offers a realist's path toward a more resilient America, with concrete suggestions for business leaders, politicians, educators, and citizens."

—Dani Rodrik, Ford Foundation Professor of International Political Economy, Harvard Kennedy School; author, *Straight Talk on Trade*

"Once again, Roger Martin has taken on a complex and thorny subject and provided compelling new insights and practical wisdom. *When More Is Not Better* shows what will truly set up our economy for long-term success: a better balance of efficiency and resilience. And it's also the prescription we need as individuals. A must-read for our time!"

—Arianna Huffington, founder and CEO, Thrive Global

"Roger Martin is my generation's Peter Drucker. He enables us to see beyond the traditional boundaries of business theory to the bigger system at play in our efficiency-obsessed world. And, like Drucker's, his prescriptions are clear, realistic, and practical."

—Jim Hackett, President and CEO, Ford Motor Company

"Martin shows how leaders fall short of achieving effectiveness because they confuse effectiveness with efficiency. Why? Because it's what prevailing organizational norms teach them about how to win—but only in the short term. Shortchanging your employees and customers by giving them less isn't the path to making your organization more effective. Martin guides you to frame your organization within a dynamic, complex system where adopting a less efficiency-obsessed and more human-centered approach results in the lasting, sustainable prosperity that it desperately needs."

—John Maeda, former President, Rhode Island School of Design; author, *How to Speak Machine*

"In *When More Is Not Better,* Martin provides important insights on the most paradoxical challenge the world is facing today: while the world has never been so well oiled and well connected, we remain more divided, with many feeling left behind and deeply frustrated. Martin not only provides a deep and clear understanding of why this is the case but also what can relatively easily be done. Thus, I was left with a feeling of optimism about bringing greater resilience to our world."

—Jørgen Vig Knudstorp, former CEO, LEGO Group; Executive Chairman, LEGO Brand Group

"Roger Martin on the fate of democratic capitalism is the perfect match of author and subject, for it allows one of the world's top thinkers to tackle one of the world's toughest problems. *When More Is Not Better* delivers a trenchant critique of the efficiency-at-any-price economic model. But it also offers something equally important and exceedingly rare: real, practical solutions. This is a timely, urgent book for business leaders, politicians, and educators everywhere."

—Daniel H. Pink, #1 *New York Times* bestselling author, *Drive, When,* and *A Whole New Mind*

"A system can be shaped to meet society's needs or it can be mismanaged so as to become unfit for any purpose. Just when America needs it most, *When More Is Not Better* brilliantly reveals where democratic capitalism has gone wrong and what new design principles we need to fix it."

—Tim Brown, Chair, IDEO; author, *Change by Design*

WHEN MORE IS NOT BETTER

WHEN MORE IS NOT BETTER

Overcoming America's Obsession
with Economic Efficiency

ROGER L. MARTIN

HARVARD BUSINESS REVIEW PRESS
BOSTON, MASSACHUSETTS

Library of Congress Cataloging-in-Publication Data

Names: Martin, Roger L., author.
Title: When more is not better : overcoming America's obsession with
    economic efficiency / Roger L. Martin.
Description: Boston, MA : Harvard Business Review Press, [2020] |
    Includes index.
Identifiers: LCCN 2020012326 (print) | LCCN 2020012327 (ebook) |
    ISBN 9781647820060 (hardcover) | ISBN 9781647820077 (ebook)
Subjects: LCSH: Capitalism—United States. | Distribution (Economic theory)
    | Industrial efficiency—United States. | United States—Economic
    conditions—1945-
Classification: LCC HB501 .M513 2020 (print) | LCC HB501 (ebook) |
    DDC 330.973—dc23
LC record available at https://lccn.loc.gov/2020012326
LC ebook record available at https://lccn.loc.gov/2020012327

ISBN: 978-1-64782-006-0
eISBN: 978-1-64782-007-7

For Lloyd Milton Martin,
wonderful father and
superb business mentor.

Contents

Foreword

Roger Martin turned in the final draft of this book on January 19, 2020, right around the time that most of us were first hearing about the novel coronavirus and first finding ways to believe that it posed no great threat to our lives or plans. Two months later, most Western nations were in lockdown and almost everything about the future was suddenly unknown. As I write these words, confined to my apartment in New York City, the national death toll from COVID-19 is approaching 20,000, and tens of millions of our fellow citizens are facing financial ruin.

Yet one of the most promising reactions to this global catastrophe has been the growing realization that it offers us a once-in-a-lifetime chance to change things—big things that seemed immutable just a few months ago. Things like the nature of American capitalism and democracy. Martin's book does not mention the coronavirus, yet it is the most essential book I know of for building a better postpandemic America, with important lessons for all Western democracies.

Martin shows us how the mental model we've been using to think about our economy is wrong, disastrously wrong. The economy is not a machine that experts can fine-tune for maximum efficiency. It is far more productive to think of it as a complex, dynamic system, like a vast garden, within which we can all thrive if we tend it properly. Among the most important things we can do is ensure that everyone has a chance to sow and to reap; that everyone has a stake in the garden's success. Martin takes us on a tour of political, economic, and intellectual history to show us how the American economy became the envy of the world by the mid-twentieth century, and how it lost its appeal as it lost some of its fairness and inclusiveness by the early twenty-first century.

Martin is well placed to guide our thinking about the big reforms that we will be considering in the coming years. He's a Canadian who was educated in the United States, lives here now, and admires America for its astonishing accomplishments and future potential. He's one of the world's leading professors of strategy, with a keen understanding of the corporate world, a deep respect for the power of free-market capitalism, and a sharp eye for the ways that capitalism, democracy, and civil society change together over time. In addition, he has spent the last decade seeking ways to improve democratic capitalism. In 2013 he initiated a project on the future of democratic capitalism at the Martin Prosperity Institute (MPI), a think tank at the University of Toronto's Rotman School of Management devoted to improving democratic capitalism as it faces competition from nondemocratic forms of capitalism and doubts from a rising generation unimpressed by what it has seen so far.

In 2014 I had the great fortune to be selected as a Fellow at the MPI, where I and six other researchers met and collaborated over the course of five years to explore ways to strengthen democratic capitalism—to make it simultaneously more dynamic and more fair. This book is the most important of many works that emerged from those discussions. It represents Martin's best thinking about how we can cultivate the best garden.

The COVID-19 crisis, along with its incalculable losses and disruptions, also gives us a once-in-a-lifetime chance to rethink the foundations of our economy and society. But to seize that chance we must improve our thinking—our mental representations of the systems that need changing. The book you are about to read will do that.

Jonathan Haidt
New York University, Stern School of Business
April 10, 2020

Introduction

A System Out of Balance

"Money really stresses me out. As a teacher, I only get paid ten months of the year and I don't have enough savings to make it through the whole summer. All I think about is how I'm going to pay the electric bill or my mortgage. I start to think of the extra shifts I have to take at the restaurant and that horrible feeling when a student of mine recognizes me. I live paycheck to paycheck. I just don't get it. I have a master's degree. I thought I did everything right. How did I get here?"[1]

Those were the sobering worries of Sarah, a forty-two-year-old kindergarten teacher in Charlotte, North Carolina. "When I was a little girl, I just wanted to be a teacher," she recalled, with equal measures of passion and wistfulness. She earned undergraduate and graduate degrees in education in her native state of New York before moving to North Carolina to pursue her career dream. But as much as she loved teaching her kindergarten kids, she found the economics of doing so in the modern US economy to be more challenging than she had ever imagined growing up, especially now that she was a single mother.

Sarah is not alone. Amy, a thirty-two-year-old yoga instructor working in Shreveport, Louisiana, had the same sense of

1

frustration: "I grew up understanding the American Dream as: you get your education and do what you love, and you can make a living out of it. I just don't think it's realistic."

My colleagues and I met Sarah and Amy in the fall of 2015, a third of the way through the Martin Prosperity Institute's six-year project on the future of democratic capitalism in America. As part of the institute's overall work, we conducted in-depth interviews with Americans like them around the country, across a wide variety of occupations, to better understand what they thought about their country and its political economy. We excluded people in the top 10 percent of the income distribution, because we were interested in how Americans outside that top bracket—the vast majority of the population—were experiencing America's system of democratic capitalism. The annual household incomes of the people we interviewed ranged from $25,000 to $110,000, with a median of $75,000—regular Americans.

Other interviewees included Matt, a thirty-three-year-old Haitian-born Miami fireman, who worked enthusiastically on the side as a bail bondsman; Kira, an effervescent twenty-seven-year-old croupier in Saint Louis, Missouri; Ryan, a forty-year-old training manager and proud father of three in Salt Lake City, Utah; Linda, a thirty-year-old registered nurse in Hoboken, New Jersey; and Dan, a fifty-year-old truck driver based in Morristown, Illinois.

Our goal for this research was to go deeper with fewer Americans, rather than seek quantitative significance using a formulaic set of questions. We interviewed and listened to each subject for hours, to learn how people were experiencing economic life across America, across many regular American occupations. Our agenda was to listen to our subjects' thoughts and gauge their emotions. We called it the Persona Project, and we came away from it with two clear findings.

The first, as exemplified by Sarah and Amy, was that people didn't feel that the economy worked for them. Sarah struggled to make ends meet for her and her five-year-old son on $55,000 a year, and Amy had largely given up. Nurse Linda was similarly dispirited: "Right now, my student-loan bill every month is one-sixth of my salary . . . I was promised an amazing job with an amazing salary. Then when I actually get out of school, I'm working in a job that pays way less." Not everybody was entirely negative, but the emotions ranged from discouraged to ambivalent.

The second finding was that people were decisively disengaged from politics. As Ryan put it: "I have to admit that I'm not a fan of politics. I'm not a fan of contention. With government and politics, I tend to check out, because when I look at it, the debates seem to go on between individuals and nothing gets done." Kira volunteered: "My interest in politics is very limited, more because I feel like there's so much to the game that I'm just not aware of." Linda opined: "I hate saying this, but I am not that interested in politics."

On the whole, our subjects were both perplexed and sheepish. They couldn't figure out why following what they thought of as the American economic success formula wasn't resulting in the kinds of favorable outcomes it was supposed to. And they were somewhat ashamed to have opted almost entirely out of the political process. They knew they should stay involved, but they felt minimal confidence that making the effort would indeed make a positive difference.

Concern for the Future of Democratic Capitalism

Their responses got me increasingly worried for the future of America's much lauded combination of democracy and capitalism. Simply put, the democratic part of the combination means that a majority of voting citizens determines who populates the government, which sets the rules for the functioning of the country and its economy. The capitalist part ensures that the means of production are largely in private hands and that markets allocate resources based substantially on supply and demand. For democracy *and* capitalism to thrive together, Americans like Sarah, Amy, and the others we interviewed must consent to it, as they traditionally have done. But for that to continue, they need to feel that capitalism is working for them—because otherwise the possibility exists that they will use their voting power to choose some other way to allocate resources and manage production.

That is why business executives and political leaders should be deeply concerned by the findings from the Persona Project. Sarah, Amy, and the others have every right to be disheartened and confused. Throughout the first nearly two and a half centuries of America's existence as a sovereign state, most citizens experienced an advance in their economic status in the overwhelming majority of those years. Based on that trend, Americans have, unsurprisingly, used their votes throughout the years to support and perpetuate capitalism as America's economic system. But that consistent economic advance has stalled, and has been for a longer period than ever before in American history.

It was only in 1947 that economists working at the US Census Bureau, started tracking median family income.[2] From the middle of the Great Depression until 1946, only the mean (or average) family income was officially tracked. The key difference is that the mean family income is inflated by the presence of very high-end incomes at the top of the income distribution. For example, if suddenly every million-dollar earner magically started earning $10 million instead, the mean (total dollars earned divided by number of families) would increase while the median (income of the middle family in the entire distribution, with an equal number of families earning more and less) would remain unchanged.

For the purposes of thinking about the functioning of democracy *and* capitalism in combination, the median family income is particularly important because the median family is, in some sense, the swing voter. To earn 51 percent (or more) of the vote in order to get democratically elected, a political party needs to satisfy the median family—not literally that family, but the families in the income band around the median. If these families don't feel that the existing system is working for them, then in due course, the voters in those families will help tip 51 percent (or more) of the electorate toward voting for something else.

In the twenty-nine years from the first year that it was tracked, in 1947, through America's bicentennial, in 1976, the real median family income in America grew at a healthy annual compound rate of over 2.4 percent, meaning the median family was exactly twice as well off economically in 1976 as in 1947—that is, doubling in one thirty-year generation. This is the kind of long-term, sustained growth that made the American system of democratic capitalism the most effective in producing broad prosperity during the country's first two hundred years. However, no such doubling happened. In the forty-two years following the bicentennial, the growth in median income fell to an anemic 0.6 percent per year, meaning that the median family was only 31 percent better off after forty-two years—less than one-third the progress in almost 50 percent more time. That is, median income rose by 100 percent in twenty-nine years and then by only 31 percent in the subsequent forty-two years.[3]

It is instructive to compare this post-1976 economic performance with that in America's darkest historical economic time: the Great Depression. This was the lengthy economic downturn in which half the US banks failed, unemployment hit almost one-quarter of the workforce, and the stock markets plummeted by 70 percent. American families—and their counterparts worldwide—worried that the economy would never come back. In the depths of the Great Depression, military veterans actually marched on Washington in protest for the first and only time in history.

Two features of the current stagnation are different and worse relative to the Great Depression. First and very surprisingly, the stagnation of middle incomes was of shorter duration during the Great Depression and recovered more quickly after the downturn compared with today. It would be nice to know what the median family earned for this comparison, but we have to rely on mean income before 1947—and while the mean isn't as perfect a measure for our purposes, it is still revealing. It took only ten years from its peak in 1929, through the worst depression in American history, for the average American income to recover its losses. In only another two more years, thanks to spectacular economic growth in 1940 and 1941 spurred in part by World War II spending, it grew a further 29 percent. That is to say, despite the country experiencing the worst depression in its history, it took only twelve years for the average American income to grow 29 percent from the predepression peak. Remember it took forty-two years—over three times as long—for the median American income, post-1976, to grow just 31 percent.

What's more, the average American family of 1929 had to wait only a further three years, after the United States entered the war—for fifteen years in total—to double its income, even taking into account the huge trough of the Great Depression. In stark contrast, on the current trajectory, it would take the median 1976 American family one hundred years to double its real family income—a span covering more than three generations. In fairness, the Great Depression was a much more painful experience in its worst years, with the average family enduring an unprecedented 29 percent decline in earnings from 1929 to 1933. The worst declines the 1976 median family faced were comparatively mild:

7 percent (1979–1982) and 8 percent (2007–2012). But with perseverance through the steep drop, the 1929 family ended up doing so much better, so much faster than the 1976 family has done and will likely do.[4]

Second, and perhaps more important, the Great Depression hit the incomes of the top-earning Americans more severely than it did those of average Americans. This meant that the American electorate could see itself relatively united in a painful economic situation, with the rich taking a bigger hit than the average worker. Nothing could be further from the truth in the current economy. While the median family is stagnating as never before, the top 1 percent (and 0.1 percent and 0.01 percent) are doing better than they have ever done in American history—and there's no sign of that stopping (see figure I-1).

FIGURE I–1

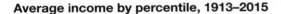

Average income by percentile, 1913–2015

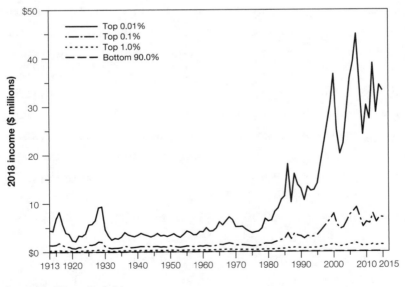

Source: World Inequality Database.

You could argue that it is perfectly fine that the rich are getting richer if their doing so helps the economy grow and if that economic growth flows to those less well-off. And you might be right if indeed the growth were robust and did flow that way. The trouble is, the data shows that most of the historically anemic growth of the past few decades is in fact being captured by the wealthy Americans that we're supposed to credit with creating it.

For starters, at around the same time that the incomes of top earners began accelerating in the late 1970s, economic growth slowed. Annual US GDP per capita growth slowed from an average of 3.24 percent in the forty-two years leading up to the bicentennial to an average of 1.75 percent in the forty-two years that followed—a 46 percent reduction in growth rate.[5] The drop in the growth rate is not in and of itself surprising or highly alarming. It is always difficult for the richest country in the world to maintain high levels of GDP per capita growth for exceedingly long periods of time, and America kept it up for an impressively long time.

More worrisome is where the growth has gone. The overall payoff profile has changed dramatically since the same approximate time. As late as 1980, the rule in the American economy was that the poorer you were, the more you benefited from growth in the American economy: Americans in the lowest fifth percentile did better than those in the tenth who did better than those in the twenty-fifth who did better than those in the fiftieth who did better than those in the seventy-fifth who did better than those in the ninetieth who did better than those in the ninety-ninth. That is, economic growth in 1980 was an equalizing force. By 2014, this relationship had flipped entirely: the poorest benefited least from growth, and all the way to the 99.999th percentile, the richer you were, the more you benefited.

Other data confirms this pattern, and perhaps there is no better illustration of how the average workers are losing out than the dramatic shift in the relationship between productivity growth and wage growth of nonsupervisory workers—the regular Americans we interviewed. Historically, up through the mid-1970s, there was an extremely tight relationship between productivity growth and wage-compensation growth. If workers were more productive, their pay went up proportionately, an outcome that spread the rewards of growth broadly, because economic growth and productivity growth are tightly coupled. For example, between 1948 and 1972, productivity grew 92 percent and wage compensation 88 percent—and they tracked each other closely each year. That meant that if workers produced more economic output for their employers, they were compensated with increased wages mirroring almost exactly the increase in output—fairness in the extreme. In 1972, however, that relationship broke up, and between 1972 and 2018, while productivity grew by 84 percent, growth in wage compensation barely budged, growing just 13 percent, or 0.25 percent per year for forty-six years (see figure I-2).

And what was once a sterling feature of the American experience, economic mobility in the land of opportunity, has ground to a halt. Strong improvement in mobility in the 1940s and 1950s gave way to slower improvement in the 1960s and 1970s, and to slight decreases since. It is now harder than it was fifty to eighty years ago to get from the bottom quintile of the income distribution to the top quintile in one's lifetime.[6]

Before discussing the implications of this data further, it is important to acknowledge that not all economists trust the numbers I have cited. And there is certainly scope for debate. For instance, you can argue that the middle class is faring better than it appears to be from the family-income numbers, because its members are getting more value per dollar of real income. The idea here is that the prices of many goods, especially those based on digital technology, such as computers and smartphones, are falling so fast that consumers are getting considerably more value for a dollar of spending on such products than they did five, ten, or twenty

FIGURE I-2

Productivity growth and hourly compensation growth in the United States, 1948–2018

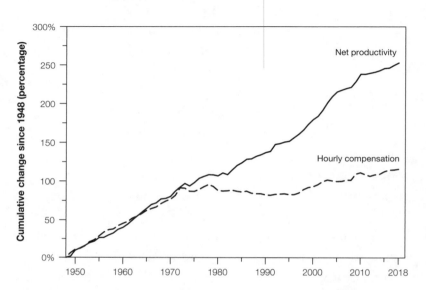

Source: Economic Policy Institute analysis of unpublished total economy productivity data from the US Bureau of Labor Statistics.

Note: Compares wages and benefits of production/nonsupervisory workers in the private sector and net productivity of the total economy. "Net productivity" is the growth of output of goods and services less depreciation per hour worked.

years ago. For this reason, many economists believe that the official adjustments made to determine "real income" (i.e., inflation-adjusted income) have had the effect of discounting current income levels by too much.

This is a reasonable point to make. My 2019 MacBook Pro is certainly more powerful than the Macintosh Duo that I owned in the early 1990s. And the MacBook Pro cost a lot less. Unquestionably, I am better off on both counts. To reflect these kinds of changes, economists apply what they call a "hedonic adjustment" to the value of my MacBook Pro, thereby revising (upward) the change in my real standard of living. With these kinds of adjustments rather than the official ones, so the argument goes, the real median family income would show a greater increase since the 1970s than the official numbers suggest, reflecting how much technology has enriched us all.

But I am not entirely convinced. To begin with, hedonic adjustments are typically pegged to a given point in time. If we take 1976 as the reference point, we might find that with the new adjustments the median income growth has fallen from 2.4 percent annually to, let's say for the purposes of argument, 1.2 percent instead of the official 0.6 percent. Fair enough, but if we are going to make hedonic adjustments, should we not also make them for the period before 1976? Across all eras, not just the recent one, competitive forces have worked to improve the average value-to-cost ratio of goods in general across the economy, so we might well find that our 2.4 percent growth rate should actually be something like 3.5 percent, and going from that number to 1.2 percent would still be a steep drop. What's more, everybody benefits from the hedonic-adjustment effect, which makes the high-income earners' true income higher as well—although the hedonic benefit is proportionately greater for the middle-income family, because it spends more of its income and saves less.

Other economists adjust the median family income numbers upward for items such as the changing size of households and the effects of progressive taxation, transfer payments, and health benefits. But even the most heroic assumptions only raise real median income growth from 0.6 percent to 1.1 percent over a comparable period.[7] Still other economists adjust the share of the top income earners downward by attempting to broaden income to include more sources not captured in the standard analyses. That lowers the degree to which the share of high earners has increased, but not by much.[8]

I do applaud the efforts to make sure that we are looking at numbers that are more representative rather than less representative, but the adjustments don't change the fundamental story of the standard public data and of the Persona interviews, which is that American democratic capitalism is more vulnerable than it was during the Great Depression.

Back then, when many of the world's major developed countries voted for fascism, communism, or socialism over capitalism, Americans stuck with capitalism, although they did shift quite significantly leftward, seeing President Franklin Roosevelt's New Deal as the best way to tackle the economic crisis of the time. And the fact that American capitalism rebounded so strongly from the 1929 crash and its immediate aftermath reinforced belief in the great American dream that hard work and passion will deliver economic and social rewards. If America could come back so strong, it must surely be doing something right, though the great collective effort of World War II played an outsize role in the recovery.

But this time, if and when discontented Americans like Amy and Sarah do reengage with democracy, it's by no means clear that they will vote to stick with the capitalism part of the American model. The 1970s represented the first protracted stumble after the recovery from the Great Depression, with two oil-price shocks and a nasty recession mid-decade. Had recovery from those challenges been as strong as that in the late 1930s and 1940s, no doubt faith in the system would once again have been vindicated. Instead, as the data shows, the post-1970s decades have been, for Americans like Amy and Sarah, a slow drip feed of disappointment and frustration.

In this environment, a more sinister narrative about capitalism has been taking root. Capitalism is no longer unambiguously about everybody working hard and getting ahead—it is about the benefit of overall economic growth flowing so disproportionately to rich people that there just isn't enough left for average Americans to consistently advance. If the little that does trickle down isn't enough to keep Amy and Sarah afloat, then sooner or later they will wonder why they trust the management of the economy to Wall Street CEOs and Beltway politicians and policy wonks. And then they will surely reengage with the democratic part of the US system—probably with dramatic and potentially harmful results.

To be sure, it is always tempting to look for a clear, easily identified whipping boy—a bad president, an atrocious piece of legislation, callous Wall Street, venal hedge funds, the unfettered internet, runaway globalization, or self-absorbed millennials. While no one of these can be held responsible for the yawning inequality of the US economy and the alienation that it engenders, many actors have played a role. It has taken almost half a century of both Democratic and Republican presidents and houses of Congress to get us to the current point. And if numerous actors are in part responsible, then we have to ask—given all that the data shows—whether there may be a fundamental structural problem with democratic capitalism. If so, can we fix it?

Ensuring the Future of Democratic Capitalism

My book is an attempt to do just that. In it, I will argue that the problem with American capitalism is rooted in a model of the economy that, over the past four-plus decades since America celebrated its bicentennial, has increasingly shaped how we think about and make collective decisions concerning the economy. This pattern of thinking and its resulting actions have produced progressively more problematic outcomes—systematically rising inequality and fragile systems among them—that are starting to fracture the once solid combination of democracy and capitalism.

The model in question holds that the economy is really a machine, a machine that can be optimized by breaking it into its constituent parts, optimizing each, and adding them back together to make an optimally running whole. Further, the machine can be made ever more perfect by pursuing increasing levels of efficiency, by which the desired outputs are created with the least possible inputs, in each constituent part. Since the definition of efficiency is rather abstract, our model of the economy uses proxies to measure and thus pursue the goal of maximal efficiency.

That model of the perfectible machine, with the attendant goal of efficiency, with its progress measured using a set of proxies, was intended to produce a big bulge of economic outcomes in the middle, with a tapering on the upper and lower ends. For families, that means a large middle class and smaller groups of both richer and poorer families. Across that distribution, the theory goes, the families on the richer end should pay substantially higher taxes in order to mitigate hardship experienced by families on the poorer end. More important, as the economy grows, everybody's income should grow, shifting the whole distribution in a favorable direction. That is, the poor families get less poor over time, the middle-class families get more prosperous, and the upper-end families get richer still. The same distribution, by the way, holds for companies. Most in an industry will experience average performance, with some big winners at the top end and some at the bottom end who struggle to stay in business.

I'll show how the evidence increasingly suggests that the output of our economic machine hasn't been producing either the assumed distribution or the favorable movement, and that it hasn't done so for some time. Instead, the bulge in the middle is slowly but surely shrinking and the prosperity of a vast majority of families is no longer moving smartly upward. Perhaps more worrisome, while government policies should be intended to serve the many for the long term, they are being gamed by interested parties to ensure that they serve the few in the short term, with damaging impact over the long term. The Persona Project respondents could feel this. To them, they were outsiders and others were playing the game to their own advantage, and to the respondents' disadvantage.

These outcomes are systemic, and without a fundamental shift in how we manage the economy, they will get only more out of alignment with our hopes and assumptions. I believe that this shift needs to start with abandoning the perfectible-machine model of the economy. We should instead understand the economy in more natural terms, as a complex adaptive system—one that is too complex to be perfectible, one that continuously adapts in ways that will almost certainly frustrate any attempts to engineer it for perfection.

In addition, rather than striving singularly for ever more efficiency, we need to strive for balance between efficiency and a second feature: resilience. A system is resilient to the extent that over time it can adjust to its changing context in ways that allow it to continue functioning and delivering its desired benefits. In the depths of the Great Depression, American democratic capitalism was resilient. It shifted, adjusted, and adapted to the shocks to its core, but it maintained the combination of those two features: democracy and capitalism. In many other developed countries, democratic capitalism was not sufficiently resilient to survive and was replaced by fascism or communism. More recent inattention to the resilience of our democratic capitalist system—thanks to the singular and obsessive pursuit of efficiency—has jeopardized that combination.

These reflections will be presented and expanded in the first part of the book, which consists of four chapters. I start in chapter 1 by explaining the critical role of models in shaping our actions. In chapters 2 and 3, I describe how the problematic changes in the functioning of democratic capitalism have resulted from our current model. In chapter 4, I offer an alternative model, that of the economy as a natural system in which we need to balance the pursuit of efficiency with the achievement of resilience and recognize that the economy can never be perfected, only improved.

In the second part of the book I turn from problems to solutions. In chapter 5, I lay out a set of comprehensive design principles that should inform the solutions so that they all drive toward a comprehensive and consistent fix. Then in chapters 6 through 9, I provide actionable and specific agendas for business executives, political leaders, educators, and citizens, respectively, who want to take small, medium, or big steps in doing their part to save American democratic capitalism. In these four chapters, I present many examples of wonderful Americans who are already taking productive steps in the defense of the future of American democratic capitalism.

I have attempted to take a distinctive approach to solutions. First, the space I give to solutions—approximately 57 percent of my book—is unusual in the context of books on the political economy. Such books typically dedicate 80 percent of their space to documenting the problem and only 20 percent to solutions. Second, I restrict my suggested solutions to prescriptions that are already in place. They may come from a different context or jurisdiction. But they are not theoretical; they are actual. They aren't speculative; they are demonstrably doable—because they have been done! I believe in the adage of science-fiction writer William Gibson: "The future is already here—it is just not evenly distributed." The task is to get solutions that are already out there and that are working, to make them more evenly distributed. And that, essentially, is the call to arms of my conclusion in chapter 10.

Let me finish on a personal note. This book is not inspired by any sudden revelation. The findings of the Persona Project are just the confirmation of ideas about tensions at the heart of the American system that have been nagging at me in my nearly four decades working at the intersection of business strategy, economic policy, and business education.

The bicentennial, which more or less coincided with the beginning of a sustained reversal of democratic capitalism's performance in America, took place during the summer between my freshman and sophomore years at Harvard College, where I was studying economics. I graduated in 1979 and journeyed across the Charles River to take an MBA at Harvard Business School. Within short order, I was working with a group of business-school colleagues to build a large global strategy firm that advised the CEOs of large companies in America and around the world—and I have advised CEOs on strategy ever since. One of those business-school colleagues was Professor Michael Porter, with whom I collaborated on his country-competitiveness work leading up to and following the publication, in 1989, of his magnum opus: *The Competitive Advantage of Nations.*[9]

In 1998, I moved back to my Canadian home to become a business-school dean and served in that capacity until 2013. While doing so, I was asked by the leader of our government to serve as founding chair of a government-funded economic think tank, the Institute for Competitiveness & Prosperity, which I did from 2001 to 2013. Since stepping down as dean, I have chaired the aforementioned Martin Prosperity Institute, a foundation-sponsored think tank working on the future of democratic capitalism. It has been during this period that the ideas presented in this book have come together to form what I suppose can be seen as our manifesto for what it will take to save democratic capitalism from itself. The marriage of democracy and capitalism has been arguably the greatest force for good in history, giving the creativity and enterprise of talented individuals the freedom to generate value in which all of us can share. History also shows, however, that its continued survival cannot be guaranteed, if we do not show the system our respect.

I hope this book will help save democratic capitalism from itself.

Part One

PROBLEM

Chapter 1

The American Economy as an Efficient Machine

Professor Wassily Leontief and I almost overlapped at Harvard University. Leontief, who won the 1973 Nobel Prize for Economics, left Harvard in July 1975 to join the faculty of New York University, and I arrived at Harvard two months later, in September 1975, as a freshman in the undergraduate college. In point of fact, I had no idea at the time that Leontief existed, or that he had won the Nobel two years earlier, or that I would go on to study economics, something he had done a half a century earlier.

The son of a Russian economics professor at the University of Saint Petersburg, Leontief entered his father's university, renamed the University of Leningrad in the wake of the Russian Revolution, at the age of fifteen to study his father's discipline, and graduated with the Soviet equivalent of a master's degree at age nineteen. He chafed at the restrictions on academic freedom imposed by the newly created Soviet Union and, having convinced the Soviet secret police that he was dying of cancer, was allowed to leave the country to pursue his PhD in Germany.[1] After completing his studies in Germany, he emigrated to America in 1931 to continue his endeavors at the National Bureau of Economic Research and to teach economics at Harvard University.[2]

In 1949, he began the work that would earn him the Nobel Prize twenty-four years later. He was interested in how the various pieces of the US economy worked together and, in due course, developed a technique for dividing the US economy into five hundred sectors, each of which could be linked to the others by modeling the inputs into and outputs out of each. He wove together these constituent "input-output tables," as he called them, to describe the entire US economy.[3] This work was seen as pathbreaking and became sufficiently influential across the field of economics to earn Leontief the Nobel Prize.

To Leontief, the US economy was a very big, complicated machine, fundamentally not unlike a car. A car has many subsystems—power train, steering, cooling/heating/ventilation, entertainment, safety, and so forth—each of which can be understood independently and then pieced together to produce the desired vehicle with the desired characteristics. Across the operation of that vehicle, the input-output equations are clear. When you push the gas pedal, the car speeds up. When you slam on the brakes, the car comes to a halt. As with a car, the inputs and outputs of the various subsystems of the economy could be mapped out and understood. Because he saw the economy as an understandable and analyzable machine, Leontief was a fan of planning, and during the economically challenged 1970s he argued that national planning might be the only hope for US economic policy.[4]

Though he left Harvard in 1975, Leontief's legacy remained. My introductory economics professor, the late Otto Eckstein, used the increasing power of digital computing to create the most sophisticated computer model of the US economy of that era, an extension and enhancement of Leontief's input-output work. In fact, Eckstein was a bit of a sensation, because in 1969 he had cofounded a thriving and influential business called Data Resources

Inc. (DRI), which provided economic forecasts based on his computer model to governments and businesses. He would go on to sell DRI to publishing house McGraw-Hill for $100 million in 1979, a staggering amount in those days for a nerdy economics professor. But the business was well worth it. Suppose you were a policy maker or government official. You would surely want to know what effect pulling a given economic lever would have on the overall machine. Eckstein's DRI made such forecasting possible. So, what was the problem?

The Power and Foibles of Models

I grew up in a tiny village and attended a regional high school in the middle of farm country in Canada but got it into my head that I wanted to study at Harvard College, across the border in the United States. I was somewhat terrified, but I survived the entry and quickly fell in love with economics.[5] While I was taking my undergraduate economics courses, I was naive as to the power of models to shape actions and the power of metaphors to drive the adoption of models.[6] I believed that the models I was being taught were descriptions of how the economy actually works. It took me a while to figure out that those models are no more than a theory of how the economy might work, if the economy were, in fact, like a car. And it is because we are all so convinced that the US economy is like a car that we stick with models like Leontief's even when those models no longer generate accurate predictions concerning the economic outcomes that will follow our interventions.

Though not cognizant of it at the time, I was exclusively taught "neoclassical Keynesian economics." The proverbial penny didn't drop for me, because the subject wasn't actually taught using that descriptor. It was taught to me as "economics"—the way the economy worked. I soaked it all in like a good little undergraduate. On our assigned reading lists, we occasionally found articles and books by University of Chicago economists, such as Milton Friedman or Robert Lucas. From what I could tell, we read these works simply to enable our professors to mock their "monetarist" thinking. It wasn't economics. It was wrong. I was not being taught *a* way to think about economics: I was being taught *the* way to do so.

I graduated into the US economy of 1979, happy to know that I now knew how the economy worked, thanks to my Harvard economics training. But perplexingly for me, I observed that the 1979 economy featured two things happening at the same time, things whose coincidence my economics education said would be "impossible." The US economy was suffering from exceedingly high inflation—11.3 percent, which was the seventh highest in the history of inflation measurement in the US economy. And it was suffering from high unemployment—in fact the seventh consecutive year of unemployment above 6 percent, a level high enough for policy makers to feel the need for significant intervention. I had been taught that it was not possible for a long period of high unemployment such as the US economy was experiencing to produce anything but slowed, not accelerating, inflation—based on the Phillips curve, which was taught as fact, at least in the Harvard economics department at the time.

At that point I had an epiphany: even though my distinguished professors taught me economics earnestly as if it were the truth (i.e., how the US economy actually worked) and warned against people who taught wrongly about the workings of the US economy (e.g., the dreaded monetarists), my professors actually taught me only one *model* for how to interpret the workings of the US economy. I feel sheepish that I hadn't figured this out before—but in my defense I was just a country boy!

It wasn't a particularly bad model. I hadn't come away from the experience thinking that the monetarists were more right than the neoclassical Keynesians or vice versa. But like all models, the neoclassical model was imperfect—and much more imperfect than my professors seemed to realize. I came away understanding that they had vastly oversold the veracity of their model, something that irks me to this day. But on the bright side, it was the best learning experience from my four years of Harvard undergraduate education, and I should be thankful for that. I learned to be careful not to have overconfidence in models—mine or anyone else's.

Long after graduation, when I came across the work of MIT systems-dynamics professor John Sterman, I gained a greater appreciation for the foibles of models. Sterman points out in his aptly titled article "All Models Are Wrong: Reflections on Becoming a Systems Scientist" that all models are flawed.[7] (This idea was first put forward in writing by statistician George Box in 1976.[8]) Because by its very nature a model simplifies the complexity of the real world in order for us to utilize the model to make decisions and take action, it leaves some things out and accentuates others, meaning that it is in some profound sense, just plain wrong. Does that mean that we should stop modeling? No. Whether we realize it or not—and often we don't—we always have a model. In fact, we can't not model. As Sterman argues: "You never have the choice of let's model or not. It is only a question of which model. And most of the time, the models that you're operating from are ones you are not even aware that you are using."[9]

I also came over time to understand the importance of metaphors in underpinning and motivating models—such as the machine metaphor of the US economy from Leontief's work. This was impressed upon me by Craig Wynett, former head of innovation at consumer-products giant Procter & Gamble. Wynett studied the subject of analogic reasoning—reasoning by way of analogy or metaphor—to better understand consumer behavior. He came to the conclusion, based on brain-science research on the subject, that human beings comprehend new things almost entirely by making an analogy to something already familiar to them. That is why metaphors are so important. An idea is generally more compelling and better understood if it is presented as being like something familiar. This is even the case if the metaphor is not presented as such but observers are able nonetheless to make an analogy to something familiar. To my knowledge, Leontief himself didn't use the metaphor of the economy as a machine, but his work can be more easily understood and is more compelling because his model strikes observers as implicitly relying on the machine metaphor.

In 1943, British Prime Minister Winston Churchill famously observed: "We shape our buildings, and afterwards our buildings shape us."[10] The same thing holds for metaphors: we select our metaphors, and afterward, our metaphors shape us. If our metaphor for our self is a lone wolf, we will feel isolated and will act alone instead of building coalitions to get goals accomplished. If our metaphor for life is a battle, then we will categorize those around us as either allies or enemies and attempt to work with our allies to defeat our enemies. If our metaphor—per Bob Dylan—is that "chaos is a friend of mine," we will embrace a chaotic life rather than attempt to organize it. If a country's metaphor for itself is a melting pot—as is America's—it will produce citizens who think of themselves first, foremost, and dominantly as Americans. Their distinctiveness will melt into the American self-conception. If a country's metaphor for itself is a mosaic—as is Canada's—it will produce citizens who feel they are a distinctive and identifiable part of a complex mosaic (e.g., as Polish Canadians, Vietnamese Canadians, Punjabi Canadians, etc.). The distinctiveness of their mosaic chip will never melt into the mass. To be clear, I am not arguing that one metaphor is inherently superior to another. The important point is that these different metaphors drive adoption of different models that produce very different outcomes.

Models in Business and Public Policy

To understand both the use and power of models in shaping democratic capitalism, it is helpful to look at a few specific models at work, identifying the metaphors that made them compelling, the outcomes they hoped to produce, their presumed cause-and-effect structure, and the proxies used to measure their effects. Let's start with an example from business.

Customer loyalty

In 1996, Fred Reichheld published a best-selling—and I think excellent—book called *The Loyalty Effect*, in which he proposed a model for business success with customers.[11] The book explicitly prioritized maintaining the loyalty of existing customers rather than overfocusing on attracting new customers. I believe that the message resonated with readers because a compelling metaphor jumped to their minds: the leaky bucket. If your bucket has a leak, you have two ways to keep it full: add more water or patch the leak.

Reichheld's insight was, in essence, that most companies choose to add water: they spend time, energy, and resources on attracting new customers, including initiatives such as reduced prices and/or special promotions for new customers that existing customers can't access. This, he argued, had the effect of making the leaks worse, because the largely ignored existing customers became more likely to defect, which made it all the harder for companies to keep their existing-customer numbers up, let alone add to them. Far better, Reichheld believed, to patch the leaks first.

That is to say, if a company had 1,000 existing customers at the beginning of a given year, but during that year lost 100 of them (that is, those customers leaked out of the bucket), the first

11 percent of growth from the remaining base of 900 customers would only get the company back to where it was at the beginning of the year—with 1,000 customers (that is, the company would merely have refilled the leaky bucket). If the company's goal had been to grow, say, 8 percent during the year in order to get to 1,080 by the end of the year, the company would now have to gain 180 new customers. Hitting the year-end goal would have been much easier had the company kept its existing customer base and needed only to acquire 80 new customers. Hence, says the customer-loyalty model, companies should focus more attention and resources on maintaining the loyalty of existing customers so that they don't have to win as many new customers to power growth.

Reichheld's book was highly influential, and many companies adopted his model. Its popularity increased when Reichheld published a follow-up article in *Harvard Business Review* in 2003 titled "The One Number You Need to Grow."[12] In it, Reichheld offered a helpful proxy for customer loyalty, which provided a practical answer to the question: How would you know whether you are engendering a level of loyalty that will result in existing customers staying rather than exiting? His proxy was intoxicatingly simple. Just ask customers to answer the following question, on a scale of 1 to 10: How likely is it that you would recommend our company/product/service to a friend or colleague? Reichheld told companies to give themselves one point if the customer answered 9 or 10, zero if the customer answered 7 or 8, and negative one for answers 1 through 6. The average score after surveying a hundred customers would be the company's Net Promoter Score. That is, if sixty answered 9 or 10, eighteen answered 7 or 8, and twenty-two answered 6 or below, your Net Promoter Score would be sixty minus twenty-two, for a score of thirty-eight. Reichheld showed that the Net Promoter Score highly correlated with future customer loyalty (and other good things like actual recommendations to friends and colleagues).

This example illustrates the core components of models: First, a desired outcome (less-expensive growth); second, a metaphor that animates a model (the leaky bucket); third, the cause-and-effect sequence intended to get you to that desired outcome (focus first on the loyalty of existing customers); and fourth, a proxy (or proxies) to measure your progress (Net Promoter Score).

In the policy realm, primary/secondary education provides another example of this sequence.

No Child Left Behind

As of the turn of the twenty-first century, there was a growing concern that, on average, American K–12 students were falling behind those of other leading nations. The desire was to improve educational outcomes for American students in order to support the global competitiveness of the American economy in the twenty-first century.

The underlying metaphor was that of the negligent parent. The cause-and-effect model built upon it was the theory that America's performance lagged because both schools and the teachers in them (the parents in the metaphor) were not being held accountable for delivering strong educational outcomes in the K–12 system, a system funded largely with American tax dollars. Teachers' efforts and attention to the task were variable, and the weaker schools had neither the will nor the power to enforce standards and improve the work of underperforming teachers. If the federal government stepped in and enforced accountability—that is, forced those negligent parents to pay attention—the variability would diminish, and the average outcome would rise meaningfully.

Results on standardized tests given to students were used as the proxy for educational outcomes. By evaluating teachers on the test results of their students and holding the teachers accountable for producing acceptable results, the federal authorities responsible for managing education would be able to identify consistently under-performing teachers and schools and have a publicly acceptable rationale for taking disciplinary actions.

While this may sound like a typically Republican approach, the No Child Left Behind Act enjoyed overwhelming bipartisan support leading to its passage in 2001, and was signed into law by George W. Bush in early 2002. The desired outcome was universally held, the metaphor helped everyone internalize the model, the model was amply compelling, and the proxy was suitably powerful to produce a relatively rare burst of bipartisan support on a major policy initiative.

We engage in the process described in these examples not because we make a particular decision to do so—but simply to create a construct to guide our decisions going forward as we manage a given system or function. As John Sterman says, modeling is automatic to humans. When we have a goal in mind, we create or choose a model to pursue that goal, and the model will indicate proxies that we can use to measure progress. We do so whether we are conscious or not of building and deploying a model. And the model we create or choose is almost always grounded in a metaphor that we can easily relate to.

With this in mind, let's look at how we think about the economy.

The Metaphor: The Economy Is a Machine

Thanks in substantial part to Leontief's outsize influence—he is more famous for having four of his PhD students go on to win Nobel Prizes than for winning the Nobel Prize himself—our metaphor for the economy is a complicated machine. We did not always view the economy as a machine. For much of American history, in fact, people viewed the economy as a black box, whose workings were mysterious and unpredictable.

It was a mystery as to why it plunged into a terrible and persistent malaise during the twenty-three-year Long Depression that began in 1873. And the mystery was repeated, along with outright terror, a generation later in the Great Depression, when stock markets fell by 70 percent, half of all banks went out of business, and unemployment soared to a quarter of American workers. All these outcomes were far more extreme than ever experienced before: American families genuinely worried about the survival of their country.

So, when policy makers and academics came up with the idea that the economy was a machine that could be steered, the idea was reassuring. Unsurprisingly, the image has continued to grow in power and influence. The Federal Reserve Board sets inflation targets and expects its monetary policies to produce exact outcomes. The Congressional Budget Office, using the latest version of the kind of computer forecasting model that Otto Eckstein pioneered, is mandated to model the fiscal impact of every piece of fiscal legislation so that Congress can "know" the future budgetary consequences of a piece of legislation before voting on it.

It is not just government that sees the economy as a machine. Business does too. A classic representation of this is found in Ray Dalio's widely viewed 2013 YouTube video, "How the Economic Machine Works." Dalio speaks with a confidence befitting the billionaire founder of the world's biggest hedge fund, Bridgewater Associates: "The economy is like a machine. At the most fundamental level it is a relatively simple machine. But many people don't understand it—or they don't agree on how it works—and this has led to a lot of needless economic suffering."[13] Dalio is hardly unique or original in using the machine metaphor.

The machine model is also integrated into job design. Companies are absolutely chock-a-block with piece-part specialists— financial specialists, tax specialists, marketing specialists, accounting specialists, production specialists, and so on. Very few employees of US businesses see their job as providing an integrative view and making integrative decisions. Each is a cog in the big machine that is their company—which in turn is a cog in the economic machine.

Businesspeople don't get this way automatically or naturally. They get trained to be this way. Business schools break down the business machine into the functional siloes (marketing, finance, operations, human resources, etc.) and teach narrowly in those siloes with little or no attempt to integrate across the siloes, all the while assuming that if someone adds up the narrow, independent answers produced in each silo, those answers will amount to a terrific comprehensive answer.

To be fair, not all business folk subscribe to the idea that business can be broken down, like a machine, into independent components. Perhaps the most influential business thinker of all time, Peter Drucker, certainly didn't buy it, simply and clearly pointing out that, "There are no tax decisions . . . There are no marketing decisions . . . There are no specialty decisions . . . There are only business decisions."[14] But Drucker notwithstanding, the business schools of America (undergraduate and postgraduate combined) pump out over half a million narrow specialists per year into the US economy—a fifth of university graduates of all disciplines combined.[15]

Economists, whether they work in a business or in the public-policy apparatus, are similarly siloed. It is so much easier to work on one piece of the machine—labor economics, industrial organization, firm microeconomics, fiscal policy, etc. (partial-equilibrium economics)—than on the challenge of figuring out how all the pieces fit together (general-equilibrium economics). That is why there are a thousand partial-equilibrium economists for every one general-equilibrium economist. It is much handier to just assume that the constituent parts add up to a predictable whole than to contemplate the complexities of the whole.

The Desired Outcome: Growth

If the metaphor is the complicated machine, to build a model on it, we must next specify what we want the economy to deliver. The answer—a steady improvement in the standard of living, or in income—is at one level quite obvious. But hidden in that answer is an assumption about how "we" benefit from economic growth. That assumption is shaped by one of the most basic mathematical models used in the natural sciences: the famous Gaussian distribution, a construct that is based on the work of the early-nineteenth-century German mathematician and physicist Carl Friedrich Gauss.[16]

You will have met the Gaussian distribution early in your life. After your very first Stanford-Binet IQ test, typically given when you are about six years old, your teacher told your parents where your result placed you on the "bell curve"—the more colloquial name we use for the Gaussian distribution. Later on, when a teacher accidentally made the test too hard (or too easy) for your class, he told you that he adjusted the grades up (or down) based on that same bell curve. If you took a statistics course in college, it was dominantly about Gaussian distributions. Later still, when you took your four-year-old daughter to the pediatrician, he explained to you where her height and weight placed her on the bell curve for four-year-old girls.

What he meant, of course, was the Gaussian distribution of children's weights and heights. It is referred to as a bell curve because when it is drawn on a piece of paper, it looks like the side view of a bell (see figure 1-1).

It is big in the middle and tapered dramatically at the edges. It is symmetrical, with both sides the same size and shape, like a proper bell. An implication of the shape and symmetry is that the greatest number of occurrences (the mode), the average of the occurrences

FIGURE 1–1

Gaussian distribution

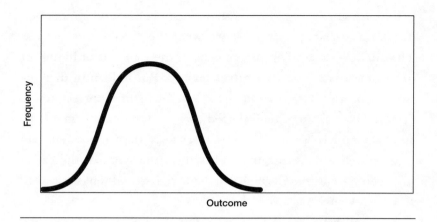

(the mean), and the fiftieth percentage occurrence (the median) are all the same. That is to say, the greatest number of observations are right in the middle, and there are equal numbers of observations to either side of the middle.

Gaussian distributions are all around us in both the natural and man-made worlds. Factors such as human weight, height, and IQ, but also things like measurement errors or slight variations in the size and weight of manufactured products from a given assembly line, array themselves in Gaussian distributions. Because they are so prevalent, they are also called "normal distributions." Our default assumption is that if we are measuring the distribution of any set of results, those results are more likely to be distributed normally than any other way.

The Gaussian distribution is a favorite of scientists because it is found so frequently in nature, and therefore the phenomenon has an apparent validity. It is not a bad default to assume that if you make a thousand observations of something—flips of a coin or sales of muffin types—the results might well follow a Gaussian distribution. (Though the latter won't!) But in addition, Gaussian distributions have handy, analysis-friendly properties. As the number of observations increases, the shape of the distribution becomes more Gaussian. This phenomenon is referred to as the central limit theorem, by which if you measure the height of 100 eight-year-old boys, the distribution will look vaguely bell-shaped, and if you measure another 9,900, the 10,000 observations will look a lot more bell-shaped, and if you measure another 990,000, the million will be perfectly bell-shaped. As you add more observations, the mean becomes more stable and the dispersion around the mean—called the standard deviation by statisticians—also stabilizes to a consistent level. Across all sorts of Gaussian distributions, 68 percent of the observations are less than one standard deviation from the mean and 90 percent are less than two standard deviations from the mean.

That is all really handy for doing analyses, so statisticians, epidemiologists, physicists, psychologists, sociologists, and economists all like working with Gaussian distributions. If they find an observation that is more than two standard deviations from the mean, they are prepared to say that this result is genuinely and meaningfully different than the mean. Imagine, for example, that the mean rate of remission from a certain kind of colon cancer is 33 percent and the standard deviation is 4 percentage points in a particularly sized trial planned for a new experimental drug. If, in that trial of patients taking the new drug, the mean remission is 42 percent—more than two standard deviations above the mean—the researchers will declare that this new drug is a genuine, meaningful improvement over the existing best practice. If the mean remission is only 35 percent, they will say that the result is not significantly different from the mean and perhaps just the product of random fluctuations.

A key characteristic of the Gaussian distribution is that it is a product of the independence of the data being observed. Going back to our four-year-old girls, if I am measuring their height, the height of each is independent of that of all the others. That is to say, if I measure the height of Sally, it tells me absolutely nothing about the height of Reshmi. Because Sally happens to be short, I can't assume that Reshmi will be tall because nature decided to take two inches from Sally and give them to Reshmi. The same holds for coin flips. If we flip a coin one hundred times and then repeat the sequence of one hundred flips numerous times, the mean, median, and mode will be a result of fifty heads and fifty tails, and the hundred-flip trials will array in a Gaussian distribution around the fifty-fifty split. That is because each coin flip is completely independent of the ones that came before. Even though the thought is fundamentally counterintuitive, if I get heads on ten consecutive tosses, I am not more likely than 50 percent to get tails on the next flip.

Given that the Gaussian distribution is so common and handy to use, it should come as no surprise that a Gaussian distribution represents our expectation of economic outcomes such as those related to income and wages. It is enshrined in our economic language, in which a core assumption is that the largest part of the population is the "middle class," which is clustered around the income mean. Most typically, we use Gaussian terminology to demarcate the middle class, often thought of as families earning between the twenty-fifth and seventy-fifth percentiles. The bulge in the middle is the middle class and the tapered end to the left represents the smaller number of poorer families and the tapered end to the right the smaller number of richer families.

To restate, then, the desired outcome of our model for the economy is economic growth, conceptualized as the Gaussian distribution of income moving steadily to the right over time, with the median income of middle-class families increasing over time

FIGURE 1–2

Desired advance in the income distribution

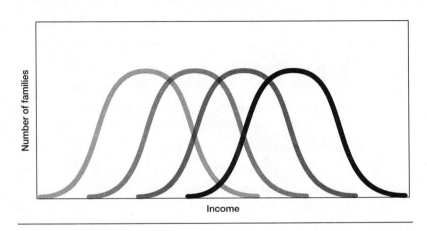

and the economic fate of the poor getting absolutely better over time (see figure 1-2).

Beyond overall growth, the Gaussian construct, in this context, also presumes economic mobility. Since independence of the outcomes is assumed, families who show up in the lower end of the distribution in a given year would have a reasonable chance of showing up in the middle or the higher end in later years rather than being stuck in their spots in the income distribution. And by extension, we imagine that other actors can, through their efforts, exhibit a similar mobility. This decade's worst-performing company can, through its own decisions and actions, turn itself into the following decade's top performer. If instead of being independent, future outcomes were dependent on current outcomes, then such economic mobility would be curtailed.

The fact that we predicate economic outcomes on a Gaussian distribution is critical to explaining why American capitalism has enjoyed consistent democratic support. The fundamental characteristic of the democratic aspect of the equation is that the government of the jurisdiction in question—America in this case—is voted into office by a majority of its citizens. In other words, 51 percent or more of voting citizens need to vote for a government for it to be charged with managing the economy. It follows, then, that if the democratic-capitalist system is operated so as to cause a Gaussian distribution of economic outcomes to shift rightward over time, the median voter—who is on average getting ever more prosperous over time—will continue to vote to support political parties that promote democratic capitalism.

This Gaussian narrative was a reasonably good description of the American political economy, at least during the first two hundred years of the country's existence. Incomes for all families moved remarkably steadily to the right in the vast majority of years, producing the largest economy in the world with by far the highest standard of living of any consequentially sized country.[17] While not perfectly bell-shaped, the family-income distribution consistently looked reasonably normal throughout the period. There has, of course, always been a longer extension to the right than to the left, because the lowest income, on the left, by definition, is zero, while the incomes for the rich, on the right, extend up into the hundreds of millions. But broadly speaking, this distortion on the ends aside, the income-distribution curve was largely bell-shaped.

However, as I observed in my introduction to this book, in the past four-plus decades, the pattern has changed dramatically for the worse. We no longer see such a consistent move rightward of a bell-shaped prosperity curve. The median family income is increasing much less rapidly than before, and the distribution of incomes is becoming increasingly skewed. To understand why this is happening, we need to reexamine our theories about what "improves" the economy as well as the proxies we employ to measure progress and guide further action.

What Drives the Outcome: Efficiency

Machines that process inputs into outputs are judged and compared according to the efficiency with which they convert the one into the other. A car that travels farther on the same amount of fuel than another car is, other factors being equal (road conditions, for instance, or weather), more efficient and therefore better by that measure than the other car. If we assume that the economy is a machine, then the same cause-and-effect sequence must apply. Greater efficiency drives growth—reflected in the progressively rightward shift of the Gaussian distribution of incomes. Based on that core principle, American economists, policy makers, and business managers have consistently optimized measures that encourage ever greater efficiency. They have been encouraged in this endeavor—and, more generally, in their beliefs—by the contributions of a handful of influential thinkers.

Adam Smith

It is an interesting and important historical coincidence that Adam Smith's *The Wealth of Nations* was published in 1776, the same year that America declared its independence from Britain. In it, Smith provides two important underpinnings for a model of efficiency. First is the "invisible hand" of an unfettered market of buyers and sellers that produces, without explicit organization, a price that generates efficient use of resources to provide the optimal quantity of goods. Second, he uses a pin factory to illustrate the technique for enhancing efficiency of production. The inefficient approach is to staff a factory with workers who independently fabricate entire pins. The efficient approach, in contrast, is to break down the pin-production process into distinct tasks—making the stem, making the head, putting the pieces together—and give each worker a single task. Through this division of labor, as Smith called it, pins would be produced much more efficiently. And if all companies in the economy would pursue division of labor and the attendant efficiency, the entire economic machine would operate more efficiently.

Smith's work was well known to the Founding Fathers, including Thomas Jefferson, Alexander Hamilton, and James Madison, who led the formulation of the US constitution and developed the basic principles of US economic policy in the quarter century following the Declaration of Independence. A full 28 percent of American libraries from 1777 to 1790 held *The Wealth of Nations*.[18] Hamilton made specific reference to the benefits of the division of labor in his 1791 *Report on the Subject of Manufactures*, lauding the "greater skill and dexterity naturally resulting from a constant and undivided application to a single object" and arguing that it "has the effect of augmenting the productive powers of labor, and with them, the total mass of the produce or revenue of a country."[19] Both Smith's invisible hand and division of labor were embraced as the economic policy of the US was formulated in this seminal period. Markets were largely left free to establish efficient prices and quantities, and as US businesses grew, they used the division of labor to produce goods ever more efficiently for those unfettered markets.

David Ricardo

Four decades after Smith, David Ricardo took the efficiency idea further with his theory of comparative advantage, arguing in *On the Principles of Political Economy and Taxation* that, since it is more efficient for Portuguese workers to make wine, thanks to their natural endowment of sunny weather, and English workers to make cloth, due to the cooler climate in which they operate, each would be better off were they to focus on their area of advantage and trade with the other.[20]

The insights of Smith and Ricardo both reflected and drove the Industrial Revolution, which was as much about innovations in processes that reduced waste and increased productivity as it was about the application of new technologies. While America immediately embraced Smith's invisible hand and division of labor, especially as the country's manufacturing sector grew in size and scale during the nineteenth century, the United States was much slower to embrace Ricardo's push for the efficiency boost that comes from freer trade. During the nineteenth century, the southern states, which were big agricultural-product exporters, wanted freer trade to make sure they had markets for their exports, while the northern states wanted protection for their nascent manufacturing industries. However, after the Civil War, America's manufacturing sector grew to rival England's, and by the turn of the twentieth century America had become both the world's largest manufacturer and its greatest exporter.[21]

That accomplishment preceded what, in hindsight, is probably the dumbest economic policy initiative in American history: the Smoot–Hawley Tariff Act of 1930. Even though America, as the world's largest exporter, had by far the most to lose in a trade war, it started one—and a monumental one at that—by dramatically raising tariffs on imported manufactured goods. Unsurprisingly, its trading partners responded in kind. The subsequent global trade war either caused or exacerbated (depending on which economic historians one chooses to believe) the Great Depression.

However, in 1947, the United States woke up to its economic place in the world and did a 180-degree turn. It took a forceful lead in pulling together chief exporting nations to create the original General Agreement on Tariffs and Trade (GATT) and continued to lead a succession of major negotiating rounds, which drove average tariffs in developed countries from approximately 25 percent in 1947 to 4 percent by 2000.[22] The efficiency Ricardo argued for in 1817 became a central US policy thrust, if not obsession, though only after 130 years had elapsed.

Frederick Winslow Taylor

In the meantime, the drive for more efficiency proceeded apace on other fronts, which brings us to Frederick Winslow Taylor. Trained as a mechanical engineer, Taylor made it his life's work to promote industrial efficiency, becoming the intellectual leader of what came to be known as the Efficiency Movement. His work was highly influential throughout the Progressive Era (1890–1920) and is encapsulated in his 1911 book, *The Principles of Scientific Management*.

Taylor is both famous (with managers) and infamous (with workers) for developing the technique of using time-and-motion studies to determine the optimal method and target time for accomplishing each task in a production process. For example, his studies would determine the optimal amount of coal with which a worker should aim to fill his shovel. Too little coal per shovel load would waste the strength of the worker. Too much coal per shovel load would tire the worker out too quickly.

To Taylor, increasing efficiency was management's most central task, as illustrated by this passage from his 1911 book: "It is only through *enforced* standardization of methods, *enforced* adoption of the best implements and working conditions, and *enforced* cooperation that this faster work can be assured. And the duty of enforcing the adoption of standards and enforcing this cooperation rests with *management* alone."[23]

Taylor's work built what is now the huge field of industrial engineering and created a focus on the use of "scientific management" to drive greater and greater efficiency.

W. Edwards Deming

A generation later, after World War II, W. Edwards Deming helped pioneer what became the field of "total quality management." Deming was born in the American heartland, in Sioux City, Iowa, at the turn of the twentieth century. He lived his first half-century in near total obscurity, working on statistical issues for the Department of Agriculture and the Census Bureau. But that all changed starting in 1947, when General Douglas MacArthur, who was overseeing the US efforts to rebuild postwar Japan, invited Deming to assist in carrying out the 1951 Japanese census. While doing this work, Deming gave a series of lectures on statistical process control and quality management that made him a legend and guru to Japanese companies attempting to become internationally consequential.

Deming created a managerial approach for organizing production so as to drive out waste and achieve both quality and efficiency, which famously influenced Toyota and what became known as the Toyota Production System. Thanks in part to Deming's contributions, which are revered to this day in Japan, the laggard Japanese auto manufacturers became the bane of Detroit carmakers, so much so that American manufacturers, auto and otherwise, came to embrace Deming's methods in the 1980s and helped drive an American manufacturing revolution. When he was awarded the National Medal of Technology and Innovation in 1987, Deming was finally a hero in his home country, thirty-seven years after Japan created the prestigious Deming Prize in honor of him.

By the final quarter of the twentieth century, America had become fully obsessed with and driven by increased efficiency. The collective belief of Smith, Ricardo, Taylor, and Deming in the virtue of efficiency has come to dominate American policy and business.

Where Does All That Leave Us?

What I hope the foregoing has established is that whether we realize it or not, our dominant model of the economy is that of a machine. The desired outcome is that the assumed Gaussian distribution of family prosperity in America moves smartly and consistently to the right over time. The cause-and-effect relationship is that more efficiency drives better functioning of the model and more progress toward the desired outcome. That implies that it is worth fighting hard to put in place fixes to the economic machine that drive it toward perfect efficiency.

Pursuit of efficiency is definitely not a bad thing. The rise in the standard of living of the average family in America from the Revolutionary War to the present is substantially the result of much higher efficiency today compared with that of centuries ago. But there is ample evidence that the pursuit of efficiency just isn't working as well now—and hasn't been for almost half a century.

The problem, as is the case in all facets of life, is that too much of a good thing is no longer a good thing. In the case of American democratic capitalism, the proxies that we have adopted for measuring and driving efficiency are turning our pursuit of efficiency into a destructive force. Let's turn to look at how and why that has happened.

Chapter 2

The Chain of Imperfection

On October 19, 2009, the *Atlanta Journal-Constitution* broke a story with the provocative title "Are Drastic Swings in CRCT Scores Valid?"[1] The CRCT acronym referred to the Criterion-Referenced Competency Tests, which were, as the article specified, "Georgia's main measure of academic ability through eighth grade." The article questioned the spectacular improvement in the student CRCT scores at a number of Atlanta-area schools, showing that the likelihood of such marked improvement was less than one in a billion.

The scores were a big deal. As the state's proxy for educational attainment under the previously discussed No Child Left Behind Act, CRCT scores represented both a stick and a carrot. It was a stick for the teachers, principals, and superintendents of Georgia schools whose students performed poorly on the test. They all received negative reviews and added scrutiny. It was a carrot for teachers whose students met their score-improvement targets, particularly those at Atlanta-area schools, where such performance qualified teachers for bonuses of $2,000 each.

When challenged, teachers, principals, and superintendents insisted that the massive improvements in scores were the result of better practices, but an investigation found that across forty-four Atlanta schools, nearly 180 educators had engaged in cheating activities, including providing correct answers to students and correcting student answers. In due course, twelve educators were criminally tried, and at the end of a long and embarrassing trial, eleven were convicted, nine of whom served jail time.[2]

CRCT scores were, again, the proxy the state used to measure progress toward the desired goal of better-educated students, using the model of greater accountability. Proxies are important, because without proxies for measuring progress, it is not possible to know whether one's pursuit of a model is succeeding or failing. However, there is a profound chain of imperfection from desired outcome to model to proxies. And that chain of imperfection can cause the use of proxies to undermine the model's ability to make progress toward the desired outcome.

The proxies that have come into standard use in the policy and business domains, proxies that have become indistinguishable in the minds of their users from the efficiency they are supposed to measure, have been converting the historically Gaussian, bell-shaped distribution of outcomes in the American economy into a differently shaped and problematic curve—known as a Pareto distribution—that threatens the future of democratic capitalism in America.

The Problem with Proxies

A model is but one representation of reality. As the saying goes, the map is not the territory. Because there is an infinite variety and amount of data in the territory—a tree here, a depression there, etc.—the map by necessity leaves some things out and highlights other things, usually determined by what we want to use the map to know. A topographical map will highlight natural terrain. A road map will highlight man-made highways. A political map will highlight national boundaries. Each is a profoundly imperfect representation of the territory.

However, after we develop and begin using a given model, we become inclined to think that the map *is* the territory. The model *is* reality—it is *the* way. We close our minds to potential flaws and to alternative, potentially superior models. The behavior of my 1970s Harvard economics professors was anything but unique. It was decidedly human. But the confusion doesn't end there. In addition to assuming that the model is the reality, we compound the problem by mistaking the proxies for the desired outcome of our model. This type of error has a name, *surrogation*, a process whereby a measure for a desired outcome becomes a surrogate for that outcome.

As Michael Harris and Bill Tayler describe in a 2019 article in *Harvard Business Review*, the recent and continuing scandals at Wells Fargo & Company provide an object lesson in surroga-tion.[3] In 2016, it was revealed that Wells Fargo branch employees had opened millions of ghost banking and credit-card accounts for customers who had never asked for them and were blissfully unaware that they existed. Later, it was found that Wells Fargo employees were doing similar unauthorized things with mort-gages and auto loans. The root cause was the bank's imposition of aggressive sales targets. The bank's goal was to have deep, "sticky" relationships with customers. Its model was to have as many ac-counts per customer as possible. Its proxy for that outcome was the number of accounts per customer. That proxy was turned into a measurement system with targets for new accounts opened per branch.

To senior management, more new accounts opened (the proxy) equaled better-served customers who had deeper relationships with the bank (the desired outcome). But what really happened was that branch employees, fearful of punishment for missing their targets, would simply open accounts without either asking or informing customers. The subsequent investigations showed that the activity had been going on since at least 2011, and parallel infractions had systematically taken place in mortgages and auto loans.[4] This surrogation of the accounts per customer with supposedly deeper customer relationships cost the bank billions in fines and restitutions, plus terrible damage to its brand and reputation. It may take decades for the bank to recover—if it ever does.

In the customer-loyalty case described in chapter 1, Fred Reichheld put forward the Net Promoter Score (NPS) as a good measure of customer loyalty. But in the minds of many users of the model, a high NPS *is* customer loyalty. There ceases to be a recognition that the NPS is just one measure, albeit a good one, of customer loyalty. That conflation leads us to take actions such as making employee compensation dependent on the employee's NPS results.

But doing that converts the map's markers into the territory, which can create problematic behavioral dynamics with employees and even customers. Two out of the last three times I bought a new car, the salesperson in question informed me that I would be receiving a survey from his company and that I should make sure to give him (yes, it was a male in both cases) a "ten on all the questions." The first time this happened (three cars ago), the suggestion was made in such an off-putting way that even though I liked the vehicle I bought on that occasion, I haven't considered buying the brand since. In this case, the company's obsession had the effect of triggering customer disloyalty, quite the reverse of what the company would want. The most recent purchase experience—including a plea similar to that made by the earlier salesman—has left me deeply conflicted about that brand too.

In the policy example from the education sector, better performance on the standardized test supposedly transformed into competitively educated students. But weaker teachers, faced with the specter of punishment for the poor standardized test scores of their students and with the lure of rewards for high standardized scores began teaching to the test, as illustrated by the Atlanta cheating scandal. That is, they stopped focusing on student learning and instead taught the students the ways to ace the standardized test, or they cheated, neither of which has much, if any, correlation with learning as desired by those who voted for the No Child Left Behind Act (NCLB) and which the scores were supposed to measure.

As a result, much of NCLB was reversed with the passage of the Every Student Succeeds Act in 2015, under the Obama administration, an act that rolled back much of the teacher testing—interestingly, again, with overwhelming bipartisan support. Of course, there were many aspects that went into the reversal, of which abuse of the testing process was only one. But the case certainly provides a compelling demonstration of what happens when proxies become goals.

Let's look now at how surrogation is contributing to the growing challenges to democratic capitalism.

Proxies in business

In business the standard management models all hold that—other things being equal—the organization with the lowest labor costs is the most efficient organization. The dominant proxy for low labor costs is the hourly labor rate paid to employees, and in order to make progress on the efficiency that derives from lower labor costs, managers will try to bring that number down. That is why companies have been outsourcing labor-intensive activities to jurisdictions where hourly labor rates are lower, whether "right-to-work" US states or foreign countries. Nuances in the quality of the output of the workers or their reliability drop out of the equation. In this way, lower hourly labor rates have become a surrogate for *increased efficiency*. In the minds of business, they are the same thing—and both an unalloyed good.

Other proxies get surrogated as well. The standard models also hold that having excess labor on the job is inefficient. Another proxy for efficiency is the elimination of slack. Exactly how many workers need to be, for example, on the retail floor to serve the expected number of customers? Exactly how many minutes should a call-center operator spend on each customer call? Anything more than the minimum is slack and hence the embodiment of inefficiency. Therefore, companies have been using ever more sophisticated algorithms to schedule workers as tightly as possible, leaving no slack for employees to serve their customers better.

It's not only labor-cost proxies that get surrogated. Most management models quite reasonably hold that lowering the procurement costs of supplied inputs makes companies more efficient. They typically measure progress by looking at the annual reduction in the procurement cost of each item. In order to increase this reduction (and thereby become more efficient) companies have been standardizing and accumulating procured items in order to create bigger "spend pools" that will strengthen their hand in negotiating lower-cost contracts with fewer, larger suppliers. Certainly, having lower costs of supplied inputs is beneficial—other things being equal. But other things aren't equal. Price is not the only feature of a supplier's value proposition that matters. For example, security of supply matters over time. Willingness of suppliers to invest in beneficial innovation can also matter a great deal over time. These considerations disappear from the equation when procurement-cost level is surrogated for efficient procurement.

Surrogation is similarly baked into the modern capital markets, where today's stock price is considered the true and complete manifestation of the value of a company. The job of executive management, therefore, is to increase that stock price in order to "maximize shareholder value." The logical imperative of this surrogation is to tie executive compensation to stock-price performance—analogous to tying teacher compensation to test scores in Atlanta.

Has that worked any better than it did in Atlanta? Recall that in Atlanta, the surrogation produced a perverse outcome, which was the absence of real student learning and the exposure of impressionable students to cheating on the part of their teachers. Consider the case of John Chambers, the CEO of Cisco Systems from 1995 to 2015. He became a billionaire by running a publicly traded company. But during his tenure Cisco shareholders suffered through two bubbles and busts. The share price peaked at $80.06 in March 2000 and plummeted to $8.60 in October 2002. It worked its way into the $25–$33 range for most of 2007 and reached $34.08 in November of that year. Following the subsequent financial crisis, it collapsed to $13.62 in March 2009, climbed to $27.57 in April 2010, fell to $13.73 in August 2011, and had recovered to $24.85 by the end of June 2014.

That was a pretty wild ride for the shareholders of record from November 2007 through June 2014. Those who hung in to the end of June 2014 experienced a decline of 27 percent in their stock price and two 60 percent drops along the way. But it wasn't so bad for Chambers. Those two big dips were handy for picking up attractively priced stock-based compensation—options in November 2009 at $23.40, and restricted stock units in September 2010 through September 2013 at $21.93, $16.29, $19.08, and $24.35. His $53 million in stock-based compensation from these five grants appreciated by about 18 percent through June 2014. If, instead of exposing shareholders to massive volatility, Chambers had overseen a steady decline from $34.08 to $24.85 during that period, his stock-based compensation would have lost about 20 percent of its value rather than gaining 18 percent. Instead of providing an incentive to improve the value of the company over time, the surrogation of today's stock price for long-term value provided an incentive to produce stock volatility at the expense of long-term value.[5] So, as with the Atlanta case, the result of the surrogation was entirely perverse. The shareholders, who were supposed to be better off, were worse off because the only thing they got more of was volatility in their stock, not appreciation of it.

The absurdity of treating a company's highly volatile stock price as a true representation of its value is not lost on everyone. Li Ka-shing is one of the world's richest people and Hong Kong's richest with a net worth of approximately $32 billion.[6] The day after Black Monday, October 19, 1987, when stock markets around the world—including Hong Kong's—plummeted, reporters asked Li how he felt suffering the single biggest one-day loss in wealth in Hong Kong's history. Li responded that he hadn't suffered any loss in wealth. The reporters begged to differ, giving as proof the diminution in value of his various public company stakes. Li responded by asking whether they could point to any shares that he had sold on or after Black Monday. They acknowledged that he hadn't. That having been established, he pointed out that he still owned actually the same number of shares in the same companies, which had the same prospects that they had the Friday before. Hence his wealth was unchanged—an argument that he could make because he didn't fall prey to the surrogation of today's stock price as equivalent to the value of a company. Unfortunately, Li is the exception, not the rule, in avoiding this particular trap of surrogation.

Business folk are in love with their metrics. It is no surprise that *Measure What Matters* has been a best-selling management book since it was released in April 2018.[7] It is an exuberant story of Silicon Valley success, written by a successful Silicon Valley venture capitalist, based on managing strictly by proxy. The thesis is that the key to success is to develop a set of proxies and then measure them rigorously and manage executive performance to those proxies. It is the ultimate testament to surrogation.

But business folk are not alone: surrogation is a trap for the people we entrust with the task of making policy, as we have seen with the Atlanta testing scandal. And this is no less true for economic policy makers than for those setting and applying the nation's educational policies.

Proxies in economic policy

Let's begin with competition policy. Antitrust legislation came into effect in the Progressive Era in order to provide a counterbalance to the "robber barons," who were creating monopolies in goods such as sugar, tobacco, steel, and petroleum products. The core idea behind the Sherman Antitrust Act (1890) and the Clayton Antitrust Act (1914) was that when a single company acquires too great a share position in an industry and secures the ability to extract disproportionate value from customers (and suppliers), it needs to be broken up in order to protect customers from exploitation. It was always understood, of course, that when companies grow to larger size, there is an efficiency advantage associated with resultant economies of scale. But those benefits couldn't be justified if customers (and suppliers) were harmed by monopoly power.

After nearly a century, this assumption was challenged by a series of revisions to the merger guidelines (in 1982, 1984, 1992, and 1997), which put in place a powerful "efficiency defense."[8] Today, even if a merger between companies in an industry creates market power that previously would have resulted in legal prevention of the merger, the companies involved can avoid that outcome by showing that the merger creates meaningful efficiencies. That is to say, if—hypothetically—Verizon and AT&T proposed a merger that would result in them controlling a combined 68 percent of the US mobile-services market (just to pick the most important market that they would dominate, and to highlight a concentration higher than the antitrust guidelines would allow a merger to produce), they could avoid having the proposed merger turned down if they could demonstrate that by combining the networks, retail footprints, and branding programs, the combined entity would be significantly more efficient.[9]

Under this efficiency defense, the trick comes in measuring the efficiency benefit of the merger in question. There are multiple kinds of efficiencies in the business environment. By far the easiest to measure are the cost savings of the type described in the hypothetical Verizon–AT&T merger: production-cost efficiencies. Much harder to measure are the longer-run efficiencies in innovation that arise out of vigorous competition (in this case efficiencies better served by keeping Verizon and AT&T independent). Because production-cost efficiencies are easily measured, they become surrogated for the overall benefit of the merger.[10]

As a consequence, both the longer-term but harder-to-measure efficiency gains that come from competitive innovation and the short-term consumer protection from a monopoly provider intent on extracting economic value from the customer are thrown by the wayside thanks to the surrogation of short-term production-cost efficiencies for overall societal benefit from a merger. This logic explains the largely hands-off policies we have seen thus far with respect to the monopoly or near monopoly of technology giants like Google and Facebook. Those virtual monopolies provide outstanding short-term efficiency—and the long-term detriments appear to pale in comparison, because they are very hard to measure.

Some commentators claim that the Republican administration of President Ronald Reagan was responsible for this profound shift in the philosophy of antitrust regulation, because the revisions began during his terms in office. However, the efficiency defense continued to strengthen under the administration of Democrat Bill Clinton. In addition, much more historically procustomer and anticorporation jurisdictions such as the European Union and

Canada have adopted similar if not stronger efficiency defenses in their antitrust policies.[11]

The shift in antitrust philosophy has had a spillover effect on capital-markets policy. There our model holds that efficient capital markets are a key to the fluid flow of capital to its highest and best use. The question, then, is how would we judge the degree to which our capital markets are—or are not—efficient? The answer once again is a sensible measure, but one that has become surrogated for societally productive efficiency and taken to damaging extremes. The narrowness of bid-ask spreads is our proxy for efficiency. The bid-ask spread is the difference between what the buyer of a financial instrument, let's use a share of stock, pays when procuring a share on a given exchange (the bid side) and what the seller of that share gets paid for the share (the ask side). If a seller offers up a share of stock for $10 and the stock exchange takes $3 for lining up a buyer to buy the share at $13, the bid-ask spread would be a relatively huge $3, or a 30 percent markup on the seller's price. If the markup were instead 3 cents, the market would be considered 100 times more efficient in terms of the bid-ask spread.

The obsessive pursuit of this proxy has had two problematic consequences. First, it encouraged the trading of all manner of sophisticated options and derivatives on the grounds that active derivative markets help reduce bid-ask spreads in the underlying securities. Hence, the huge growth in derivatives leading up to the global financial crisis in 2008–2009 was viewed as an unalloyed good—until those derivatives played a key role in causing the massive stock-market crash.

Second, and related to competition policy in general, bid-ask spreads in a given exchange tend to fall when a larger pool of stocks is traded on the exchange in question. Hence, antitrust policy has been very lenient in allowing the consolidation of stock exchanges both in the United States and around the world. This leaves more and more power in the hands of fewer large exchanges and introduces the fragility we saw in 2008–2009 when these large markets moved quickly and dramatically downward in concert. Consistent with the competition-policy argument above, this surrogation of bid-ask spreads for societally beneficial efficiency may sacrifice long-term benefits for a narrow, short-term efficiency goal.

Similarly, in trade policy, most economists and policy makers believe, per David Ricardo's theory of comparative advantage, that the more open a country's markets are to international trade, the more efficient those markets—and, by extension, the domestic economy they support—will be. The proxy for openness is the tariff level; the lower, the better, with zero being the optimal level. The tool for achieving the ultimate goal for this surrogated proxy for efficiency is the free-trade agreement. For most of the past seven decades or so, we have been busily signing one free-trade agreement after another because the zero-tariff level that they (in their ultimate manifestation) provide is equated with the efficiency of our economy.

Proxies and Their Lineage

It is both important and only fair to note that, in the main, the fathers of the efficiency-oriented intellectual traditions would almost certainly not have taken their ideas as far as we have seen them taken. Adam Smith did not argue that labor divided more ways is always better. David Ricardo did not insist that more free trade agreements are always better. And most certainly W. Edwards Deming did not argue for the utter elimination of slack—in fact, he argued for the importance of maintaining an optimal level of slack. The exception might be the considerably more doctrinaire Frederick Winslow Taylor. It is not clear from his work whether he saw a line after which he felt that too much efficiency was being pursued. Some even believe that he falsified his data to buttress his theories.[12] But it is reasonable to suggest that business managers and political leaders in the United States have, by confusing models with reality and through surrogation of proxies for goals, taken the models of great thinkers to places where those thinkers would never have gone.

The Flow Back from Proxies to Outcomes

To review, the model of the perfectible machine, driven forward by the ever intensifying pursuit of efficiency, has unleashed on the modern American economy a number of proxies whose pursuit has become indistinguishable from the pursuit of the desired outcome. That is, there is a powerful assumption that if we achieve greater progress on a given proxy, we will achieve a favorable movement in the Gaussian distribution of prosperity. Sadly, the opposite is occurring. Performance on the proxies is generating outcomes that are fundamentally inconsistent with what we want—and need—from our economy. It is producing a different kind of distribution for economic outcomes, one that is in tension with our system of democratically chosen government. That distribution, the Pareto distribution, is the subject of the next chapter.

Chapter 3

Toward a Pareto Economy

The Gaussian distribution is by no means the only distribution of economic outcomes imaginable. At the turn of the twentieth century, Italian economist Vilfredo Pareto noted that, at the time, 20 percent of Italian families owned 80 percent of Italy's land.[1] Most of the remaining 80 percent, who owned no land, farmed the land owned by their rich and often oppressive landlords. The Pareto distribution named in his honor—or Power Law distribution to most statisticians—takes the shape of the curve seen in figure 3-1.

On this curve the many poor Italians with little to no land are on the left side and the very few superrich, landowning families are in the long tapered end to the right.

Along with a very different shape, a Pareto distribution has markedly different characteristics than a Gaussian distribution. There is no meaningful mean or median in a Pareto distribution. The median is often nil—for example, the median Italian family in Pareto's time owned no land. To say the median landowner-ship in nineteenth-century Italy was zero doesn't tell one much about the overall distribution, while saying the median height of

FIGURE 3–1

Pareto distribution

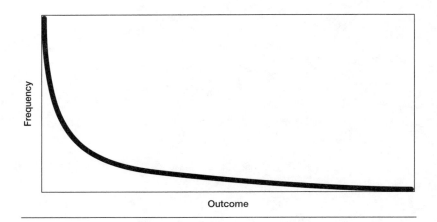

an American male is 5' 9.5" tells one quite a bit more about that overall distribution.

Also, a Pareto distribution is not stable. As discussed in chapter 1, when additional observations are added to a Gaussian distribution, the overall pattern of distribution becomes only more pronounced thanks to the central limit theorem. The addition of new data points has no such predictable effect on a Pareto distribution. They might make it less extreme, make no difference, or make it even more extreme. Often, for reasons explained below, it is the latter, but it is not necessarily so.

The key difference between Gaussian and Pareto distributions is that while independence of one observation from another is a central characteristic of a Gaussian distribution, the observations in a Pareto distribution are connected to one another. In the Gaussian distribution of American adult male height, for example, no one person's height has any impact on the height of any other male. This creates a distribution in which the tallest American male—at 7' 8"—is less than 1.5 times as tall as the aforementioned median.[2]

Now consider social media—Instagram, for example. If the distribution of the number of followers per Instagram user were a Gaussian distribution, it would be because when Instagram users decided whom to follow, they did not take into consideration the number of followers a candidate for followership already had. This, of course, is not the case by any stretch of the imagination. The number of existing followers is *a* key, if not *the* key, consideration in deciding whether to follow a person. If a person has few followers, the inference is that they are not worth following. If a person has many followers, she is not only worthy in general, she is probably worthy of following.

That is why the median user of Instagram has 100–150 followers while soccer star Cristiano Ronaldo, according to a recent count, has 218 million followers.[3] The phenomenon is called "preferential attachment."[4] I see it as attractive for me to attach to Ronaldo because Ronaldo already has many followers. In the Pareto distribution, an important dynamic is that the effect (having more followers) is the cause of still more of the effect (having still more followers), which causes yet more effect, and so on.

Since Pareto's time, many scholars have studied the dynamics and implications of Pareto distributions, including those who work in complexity theory, who note that Gaussian distributions aren't the only ones that appear in nature. Pareto distributions do as well. A favorite example for complexity theorists is the collapsing sand pile. Imagine on the above Pareto graph, the number of grains of sand dropped on a pile is measured on the vertical axis and the effect of each sand grain on the horizontal axis. If the grain of sand has no noticeable impact on the shape of the sand pile, it shows up on the extreme left side of the chart. If it causes the pile to collapse entirely, it is on the extreme right. When grains of sand are dropped on top of an existing sand pile, nothing much happens to the shape of the sand pile for thousands and thousands of drops of sand grains—hence the very tall bar on the extreme left of the

Pareto chart. But after enough grains are dropped, the dropping of one additional grain will cause the sand pile to collapse entirely—that grain is marked way out on the long, tapered end of the Pareto chart. This experiment can be run with a thousand sand piles, and the distribution will always be Pareto. The overwhelming majority of sand grains are dropped with no evident effect, and then one becomes the proverbial straw that breaks the camel's back—another great metaphor—and the pile collapses.

From Gaussian Distributions to Pareto Distributions

This matters to the fate of American democratic capitalism, because complexity scholars, including Bill McKelvey of the Anderson School at UCLA, from whom I learned this, have identified several factors that systematically push Gaussian outcomes toward Pareto distributions. Chief among them are two things: (1) pressure on the system in question and (2) ease of connection among the participants in the system.[5]

The sand pile can be used to illustrate. First, if the sand pile existed in a low-gravity context, it wouldn't collapse. It collapses only as the pressure applied by earth's relatively strong gravity accelerates that final grain down with enough force to jar enough other grains out of position to drive a total collapse. Second, if the grains of sand were not connected with one another but rather independently placed in a superstructure, the additional sand grains would not have impacts on the others and would not start a collapse. For this reason, a Gaussian distribution facing a relatively low level of pressure and relatively high costs of connection between participants in the distribution would stay Gaussian for a long period of time—so much so that we think of it as naturally Gaussian. But if more pressure is applied to the participants in the

FIGURE 3-2

Transformation in income from Gaussian to Pareto distribution

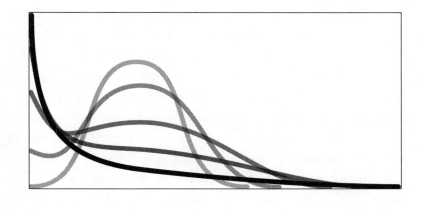

distribution and the cost of connection falls, the distribution will more quickly turn Pareto (see figure 3-2).

For the US economy, efficiency is gravity's equivalent. The obsession with ever greater efficiency, amplified by the pursuit of surrogated proxies for efficiency, has converted a Gaussian distribution of outcomes into a Pareto one. Relentless pressure on labor and procurement costs, the near elimination of slack, and the opening of markets by the General Agreement on Tariffs and Trade and the World Trade Organization have increased competition across industries. If companies fail to become more efficient in their operations, they will be driven out of business by local or foreign competitors. To this pressure is added, thanks to the efficiency defense for mergers, increasing consolidation as more and more industries turn into oligopolies or monopolies.

Meanwhile, the internet has slashed the costs of connection. Everything is more easily and inexpensively connected to anything and everything else. The internet is not the only driver of falling connection costs in the economy. The mergers of the capital-market exchanges, for example, have lowered the cost of connecting one equity pool to the next, while regulations such as the Financial Industry Regulatory Authority (FINRA) Rule 5310, which requires all trades to be routed to the market that has the best current price for the security, are forcing markets to interconnect seamlessly, thereby reducing the costs of connection to zero. With microwave towers now connecting the Chicago Board of Trade to the New York Stock Exchange, arbitrage between the two markets has become virtually nonexistent. Forced salary disclosure by the Securities and Exchange Commission of the five top-paid executives of publicly traded companies means that, for example, the compensation of our company's CEO is seamlessly connected to and comparable with the compensation of every public-company CEO in the country, meaning that if those salaries go up, there will be instant upward pressure on the compensation of our CEO.

To illustrate the impact of pressure and connectedness, let's return to the fame game introduced above. Fame has always been a competitive game. It was difficult to achieve singing stardom like that of Frank Sinatra in the 1960s or supermodel stardom like that of Cindy Crawford in the 1980s. But these were arguably smaller and more fragmented games. We didn't routinely ask who was more famous: a singer or a supermodel. It was hard to measure and compare—like apples and oranges. And the competition wasn't as intense, because the payoff for achieving standout fame in your particular discipline was lower. For example, as the most famous crooner of his generation, Sinatra amassed a lifetime fortune of $100 million. And as the most famous supermodel of her generation, Crawford also amassed a lifetime fortune of $100 million.[6]

Like much of the US economy, fame has gotten much more competitively intense and much more tightly connected. Ronaldo has ascended the global soccer mountain, which is probably somewhat more competitively intense and tightly connected than it was twenty-five years ago, but not orders of magnitude more so. But parlaying that soccer fame into ubiquitous celebrity fame is a much more pressure-filled game. If you aren't positioning yourself cleverly on social media, you are going to be left behind—and once you fall behind, it is ever less possible to catch up. Thanks to the zero cost of connection and the utterly standardized measuring stick (Instagram followers), soccer-star Ronaldo is pitted against female singer Selena Gomez, male singer Justin Bieber, wrestler-turned-movie-star Dwayne "the Rock" Johnson, celebrity Kim Kardashian, and celebrity-turned-cosmetics-mogul Kylie Jenner.

The dynamic has very tangible consequences. With his lofty standing in Instagram followers, Ronaldo earns a reported $750,000 for every sponsored post. But he has to take a back seat to twenty-one-year-old Jenner. She trails Ronaldo with (a mere!) 175 million followers, but the advertisers like her followers better than Ronaldo's, so she earns a reported $1 million per sponsored post.[7] Imagine: in a single Instagram post, she can make 1 percent of the lifetime wealth of Cindy Crawford. Two posts per week for two years would generate upward of $200 million in revenues. Given that the cost of doing so is minimal, she would—after taxes—accumulate wealth of over $100 million in less than two years on Instagram posts, while probably spending, over those two years, only about as much time as Sinatra did in one concert or Crawford did in one modeling shoot. Thanks to her fame, and her skincare and cosmetics line based entirely on that fame, Jenner is the world's youngest billionaire.

In the discussions of these Pareto outcomes in income and wealth, the two causes pointed to most often are globalization and technology. While both have indeed played a role, it is important to understand that globalization and technology are not in and of themselves the causes of the Pareto shift. While globalization has contributed to increased pressure, it is hard to see globalization as the central cause when the shift toward a Pareto distribution of outcomes was well under way by the 1970s yet most of the meaningful increase in globalization took shape much later. In terms of truly free trade, America's first consequential free-trade agreement wasn't until 1988, with Canada, and then 1994 when it was expanded to include Mexico (NAFTA).[8] There wasn't another free-trade agreement until after 2000. (The only prior one was a more symbolic than economic agreement with minor trading partner Israel in 1985.) Arguably the meaningful impacts of globalization took effect close to a quarter-century after the Pareto shift took shape. The same timing caveat has to be issued for the impact of technology on lowering the cost of connection. The first commercially successful personal computer—the Apple Macintosh—didn't make its appearance until 1984. The internet didn't come into play until the early 1990s, and smartphones until the late 1990s. E-commerce was still a new thing as of the first (and largely unsuccessful) dot-com boom at the end of the 1990s. This is a quarter-century into the Pareto shift. To be sure, globalization and technology have deepened and intensified the Pareto shift. But we can't argue that two forces that arrived at the party in question a quarter-century late are, together, responsible for the party's outcomes. The obsession with efficiency began much earlier.[9]

At a broader and more fundamental level, increases in pressure fueled by an obsession with efficiency, measured through surrogated proxies, in a context of increased connectedness, are making the distributions of outcomes in almost all spheres of economic activity increasingly Pareto, crowding out the historically Gaussian patterns that we have always assumed. It is most obvious in wealth, where the distribution is far beyond the 80–20 of Vilfredo Pareto's Italy. The richest 1 percent of Americans own almost 40 percent of the country's wealth, while the bottom 90 percent own just 23 percent. The richest American is 10 million times richer than the median American.[10] Beyond income and wealth overall, we're also seeing the distributions of job-market rewards and company profits moving smartly from Gaussian to Pareto, with fewer bigger winners and plenty left behind. To be sure, we are not there yet. But as the next few pages will show, we are systematically heading in that direction. Let's start with jobs.

The Rewards for Your Labor

It is becoming increasingly apparent that certain kinds of jobs in certain kinds of industries offer disproportionately more rewards for the people doing them. This can be seen by combining the findings of two scholars of work, one who studies the industries in which Americans work, the other who studies the kind of tasks American workers do.

Let's take industry first. Michael Porter, in *The Competitive Advantage of Nations,* demonstrated that it really matters in what kind of industry an American worker holds a job.[11] It could be an industry that sells its output in markets outside its local region (as with steel or semiconductors or pharmaceuticals) or one that does not (like hairdressing or landscaping). It turns out that the former end up clustered in only a few regions (or maybe only one) in America, because companies in these industries have the capacity to grow to great scale and they must be highly competitive to triumph over players from other regions. Hence, these companies invest more in plant and equipment, research and development, and marketing in order to prevail. In contrast, the latter are found in every region of the country, because their goods and services are needed everywhere but it is difficult if not impossible to sell outside their region. For example, with few exceptions, a hair salon will serve only its local market. About a third of US jobs are in the former, clustered industries, and the rest are in the latter, dispersed industries.

From the job-type perspective, another scholar, Richard Florida, in *The Rise of the Creative Class,* demonstrated that the content of an American worker's job really matters.[12] In particular, it matters whether the content of the job is creativity-intensive or routine-intensive. In a creativity-intensive job, the worker needs to exercise meaningful, independent judgment and decision making in order to fulfill the requirements of the job. Such workers include doctors, business executives, teachers, researchers, and police. In a routine-intensive job, the opposite holds. The worker should not exercise meaningful judgment or decision making and should instead follow a prescribed routine. Such workers include assembly-line workers, hospital orderlies, and retail clerks. Creativity-intensive jobs account for just under 40 percent of US jobs. The rest (60 percent) are routine-intensive jobs.

Unsurprisingly, jobs in clustered industries, on average, pay considerably more than jobs in dispersed industries, because the employer invests much, much more capital behind each employee, and that opens up the possibility of that employee being much more productive and earning a salary that is consistent with that higher productivity—though, as we have seen, the historic relationship between increased productivity and wage growth has weakened. Also, unsurprisingly, jobs that are creativity-intensive, on average, pay considerably more than jobs that are routine-intensive. The creativity-intensive jobs require much more formal education and higher skill levels than the routine-intensive jobs, and hence pay consistently higher wages.

Combining the two factors makes the effect more extreme. If type of industry and content of work are combined, the compensation distribution across the four combinations begins to look substantially Pareto. Routine-in-dispersed jobs (e.g., that of retail clerk) make up the largest cohort, at 45 percent of the US job market, and bring an average income that is 37 percent below the national average. Routine-in-clustered jobs (e.g., that of assembly-line worker) make up 16 percent of the labor market and bring an income 18 percent below the national average. Creative-in-dispersed jobs make up 25 percent of the labor market and bring earnings 36 percent above the national average. And in the catbird seat, the 14 percent of workers in the creative-in-clustered category earn 78 percent more than the national average. While not a perfectly Pareto distribution, it is more Pareto than Gaussian, and heading swiftly in a Pareto direction. The data for 2012 shows a markedly more Pareto shape than the data from a mere twelve years earlier, in 2000 (the earliest year for which this data set is available).

The top graph in figure 3-3 compares the overall data for these four categories in 2000, while the four smaller graphs below it break out the changes between 2000 and 2012 for the individual categories. The top of these four graphs shows that in the largest and lowest wage category, the wages have stagnated completely for twelve years, as the 2000 and 2012 boxes overlap completely. For the next category, wages at the higher end of the category (the seventy-fifth percentile) have grown marginally—the solid box (2012) extends a bit past the hatched box (2000)—while the lower bound (the twenty-fifth percentile) stays completely constant. Things get considerably better for the third category, as both the lower bound and the upper bound have increased substantially. But that pales in comparison to the progress of the highest-income category in the bottom graph. In a classic case of the rich getting richer, the lower bound increases nicely and the upper bound increases dramatically. Hence in a mere twelve years, the whole cohort has become especially well-off and much more so for its top end. Again, it must be emphasized that this dramatic divergence between the accelerating creativity-intensive workers and the stagnating routine-intensive workers has taken place in a mere twelve years, less than one-third of the working life of the workers across these four boxes.

FIGURE 3–3

Employment income by occupational and industry clusters

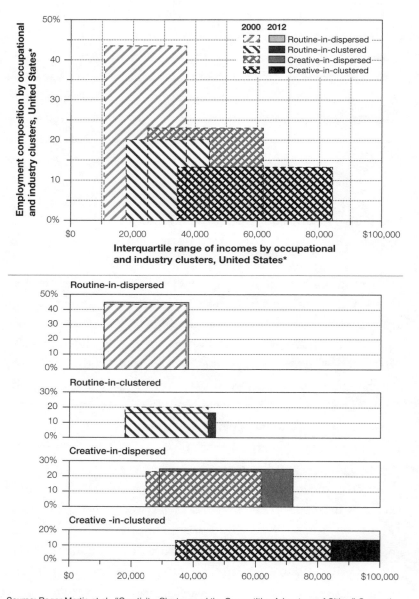

Source: Roger Martin et al., "Creativity, Clusters and the Competitive Advantage of Cities," *Competitiveness Review* 25, no. 5 (2015): 482–496.

*For all US employed wage earners, excluding those in the military and in farming, fishing, and forestry.

Pareto Distribution in Companies

Industry consolidation is increasingly common in the developed world. In more and more industries, profits are concentrated in a handful of companies. In the United States, for instance, 75 percent of industries have become more concentrated in the past twenty years, and profits have followed suit. In 1978 the one hundred most profitable US firms earned 48 percent of the profits of all publicly traded companies combined, but by 2015 the figure had nearly doubled, to 84 percent.[13] The success stories of the so-called new-economy companies are in some measure responsible. The dynamics of platform businesses, where competitive advantages often derive from network effects, very quickly convert random distributions into Pareto ones, as Instagram did with fame sorting.

But Pareto distributions are also common in traditional industries. Consider the American waste-management industry. At one time there were thousands of little waste-management companies—garbage collectors—across the country. Each had one-to-several trucks serving customers on a particular route. The profitability of those thousands of companies was fairly normally distributed. Most clustered around the mean, with some highly efficient and bigger companies earning higher profits and some weaker ones earning lower profits.

Then along came the late Wayne Huizenga, the founder of Waste Management Inc. (WMI). Looking at the cost structure of the business, he saw that two big costs were truck acquisition (the vehicles were expensive, and because they were used intensively, they needed to be replaced regularly) and maintenance and repair (intensive use made this both critical and costly). Each small player bought trucks one (or maybe a handful) at a time and ran a repair depot to service its small fleet.

Huizenga realized that if he acquired a number of routes in a given region, two things would be possible. First, he would have much greater purchasing leverage with truck manufacturers and could acquire vehicles more cheaply. Second, he could close individual maintenance facilities and build a single, far-more-efficient one at the geographic center of each region. As he proceeded, the effect—greater efficiency—became the cause of more of the effect.

Huizenga generated the resources to keep buying small garbage companies and expanding into new territories, which made WMI bigger and more efficient still. This put competitive pressure on all small operators, because WMI could come into their territories and underbid them. Those smaller firms could either lose money or sell to WMI. Huizenga's success represented a huge increase in pressure on the system.

Like a collapsing sand pile, the industry quickly consolidated, with WMI as the dominant player, earning the highest profits. Fellow consolidator Republic Services established itself as the second player, earning decent profits. Several considerably smaller would-be consolidators earn little to no returns, and lots of tiny companies mainly operate at subsistence levels. (See figure 3-4.)

The industry today is structured as a Pareto distribution, with WMI as winner-take-most. The company earned more than $14 billion in 2017. Huizenga died a multibillionaire.

That is the fundamental story of the modern American economy. Income and wealth are becoming fundamentally Pareto distributed. The pie is getting bigger, as it is supposed to. But the vast majority of every dollar of economic growth is ending up in the hands of a small minority of Americans—that is, American citizens and American companies. As a consequence, there is not enough left to move the rest of the distribution forward. The middle class (the hump of the bell curve in a Gaussian distribution) is at worst going away and at best stagnating rather than moving forward.

FIGURE 3–4

The US waste-management industry

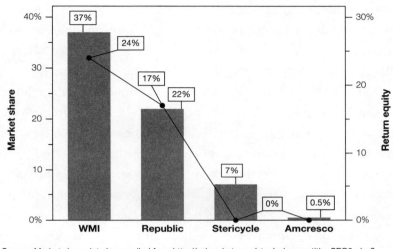

Source: Market share data is compiled from http://csimarket.com/stocks/competitionSEG2.php? code=WM; return equity data is compiled from Yahoo Finance.

Note: The bars represent market share and the line represents return equity.

But that's not the only consequence. Nature shows us that systems in which a small number of highly efficient actors dominate become vulnerable to an external change. And it turns out that this is as true for economic systems as it is for natural ones.

The Rise of Monocultures

To illustrate that point, let's take the case of the almond-growing industry. Not so very long ago, almonds were grown in a number of places in America and across the world. But some places are better than others for growing almonds, and as with most production contexts, there are economies of scale to consolidation. In this case, the Central Valley of California is perfect—totally perfect—for growing almonds. Consequently, over 80 percent of the world's almonds are now produced in this one valley.[14] This is what agricultural scientists would call a monoculture, and they are a common outcome in systems that maximize efficiency. A factory produces a single product, a single company dominates an industry, a single piece of software dominates computer systems. We remove unhelpful inefficiencies and get more productive.

But with that high efficiency comes an inherent vulnerability to shocks, with potentially catastrophic results: one extreme local event—a wind-swept fire, say, or a pernicious virus—could wipe out 80 percent of global almond production all at once. And there are knock-on effects. All of the almond blossoms need to be pollinated in the same narrow window of time, because all the almond trees grow in the same soil and experience the same weather. The huge volume of simultaneous pollination necessitates shipping in beehives from all over America for the short pollination window. There is an epidemic of honeybees dying in America, creating concerns about the US honeybee population's ability to pollinate the wide variety of plants that need the bees' busy work. One theory for the elevated honeybee mortality rates is that beehives are trucked around America for these monoculture pollinations like never before, and that this is stressful for the bees.

Rather than producing resilient ecosystems, our obsession with efficiency proxies is producing fragile monocultures, potentially vulnerable to catastrophic failure. No doubt the monocultures are efficient in a narrow sense, but that efficiency has a dark side. The problem is, we have become so convinced that efficiency-at-all-costs is a universal good that we have lost sight of its risks. We have stopped seeking dynamic balance entirely.

And we shape our infrastructure to support our monocultures. There is now an entire infrastructure designed to bring bees to the Central Valley of California and take them back to their home locations afterward.[15] Once that infrastructure is in place, it makes it considerably easier to add still more acreage of almond trees. The effect (an efficient infrastructure for almond growing in a single locale) becomes the cause of more of the effect (more almond growing in a single locale).

An almond crisis may not happen. But something like it already has. Irish farmers discovered during the seventeenth century that the South American potato grew well in Ireland's soil and climate. They also found that one particular variety, the "lumper," was more productive than any alternative food crop they could grow. By the 1840s, nearly every Irish farm was devoted to growing lumpers, which had come to account for the bulk of daily food consumption for over half of the Irish population. Then, in 1845, Irish potatoes fell prey to a water mold called *Phytophthora infestans* that decimated the potato crop. It wasn't a situation in which just some of the potatoes fell prey—virtually all did. And since potatoes were the primary source of food for most poor Irish families, the mold was responsible for the deaths (by malnourishment) of approximately 1 million of the 1844 population of 8.8 million, not to mention the emigration of a further 2 million. The devastation was so great that by the time Ireland gained its independence, in 1921, the population was still less than half its 1844 level.[16]

The Fundamental Challenge

A Pareto distribution of outcomes wouldn't be a big problem if everyone just cared about the overall growth rate. It is, to be sure, lower than it was in America's first two hundred years, but that is not altogether surprising. We expect economies to grow faster when young and to slow down as they mature. The really big problem lies in the distribution of the benefits of that growth. American capitalism requires the consent of the majority of American citizens. As I've pointed out already, if 51 percent or more of citizens experience stagnation rather than growth, they will at some point defect from capitalism. They didn't in the Great Depression, but that doesn't mean that they won't this time. Meanwhile, the grains of sand continue to fall. In a Gaussian distribution, that wouldn't matter: the independence of the occurrences provides stability—with time and more occurrences, such a distribution becomes only more stable. But economic outcomes are not independent: effects are causes of more of the same effects. So, if you are already in the top 1 percent, that position provides more opportunity to accrue still more benefits—and it is that interdependence among the grains of sand that can transform a Gaussian distribution into a Pareto one. As the effects multiply, the Pareto distribution will become only more extreme. That is the great challenge for the future of democratic capitalism. It is why we need a better model for democratic capitalism—one that recognizes it is a natural system that needs constant tweaking rather than a perfectible machine. That is the subject of the next chapter.

Chapter 4

The American Economy as a Natural System

In the spring of 2009, at a time when the global financial crisis still threatened to bring down the entire economy, I attended an event at which the dinner speaker was one of the world's leading macro-economists. He spoke confidently for about forty-five minutes on the state of the US economy and explained exactly what, in his view, Congress and the president needed to do in order to ensure the country's economic recovery.

He was the chief economist for one of the fifty organizations that Aspen Publishers polls to create its widely followed Blue Chip Economic Indicators forecast. Every month Aspen releases both the consensus (which it defines as the average of the fifty forecasters) and all fifty individual forecasts of US real economic growth, both for the current year and for the following year. I had followed the Blue Chip forecasts during 2008 and had noticed, to my subsequent astonishment, that all fifty forecasters, including of course this gentleman's organization, had predicted for every single month, up to and including the December 2008 forecast, positive economic growth for the 2008 year. They weren't exuberant—the forecasts ranged from low to medium growth—but not one had suggested that 2008 growth would turn negative.[1] In other words, as late as the last month of the fourth quarter, all fifty forecasters still had positive growth forecasts for the 2008 year, despite the fact that the economy had already shrunk 2.1 percent in the third quarter and was two months into a nearly unprecedented 8.4 percent drop in the fourth quarter of 2008—all of which produced an annual decline of 2.75 percent, one of the worst in the previous half-century.[2]

In the question-and-answer session after his speech, I was well behaved. I didn't ask him directly about his forecast, from which he stayed far away in his talk. Instead, I attempted diplomacy, asking him how he might have adjusted his forecasting model for the US economy based on the degree to which the economic implosion in the back half of 2008 caught so many economic forecasters by surprise. His response suggested that he thinks no one checks his forecasts, because he assured me that he had seen the second half collapse coming and therefore nothing about his model needed adjusting. I didn't ask why his forecasts had reflected the precise opposite. But I was left with a better understanding of why the forecasts were not going to get better anytime soon.

Five years later, the same thing happened again. In the fall of 2012, economists started to fret about an impending "fiscal cliff." This was the catchy name given to a combination of five tax increases and two spending cuts that were all scheduled to take effect on January 1, 2013, an event that the Congressional Budget Office estimated would remove $607 billion from the US economy in the first nine months of 2013. This, the CBO declared, would result in a 1.3 percent contraction of the entire US economy, which in turn threatened a resumption of the horrible downturn of the global financial crisis.[3] Federal Reserve Chairman Ben Bernanke waded in as well, calling the fiscal cliff a "massive" shock to the US economy. Economists across the country pleaded with Congress to pass legislation to counteract and avoid this terrible threat. Unsurprisingly, Congress spent the time bickering and did nothing of the sort.

And what happened? Absolutely nothing, and today the "fiscal cliff" is all but forgotten. Bernanke, the CBO, and all the hyperventilating economists and their machine models were just plain wrong—and not a tiny bit off. They were totally and utterly wrong, despite the certainty and precision with which they predicted the disasters that would ensue.

The moral of these two stories is that the economy does not work like a machine. It doesn't have independent parts that can be optimized with zealous pursuit of proxies for efficiency and that directly project local optimization to the whole system. If it did, the smart economists who invest so much time in creating macroeconomic models and formulating algorithms to describe the effects that a given cause will produce would not produce such poor predictions. It is precisely because the economy makes such fools of the experts who study it that we have to ask whether there isn't something fundamentally wrong with the highly mechanistic approaches that they take.

A more powerful and useful metaphor for the US economy than a complicated manmade machine is a natural system, like a rainforest. There's an irony in that while America is entranced with Amazon Incorporated, with its machine learning and algorithms, the country would actually learn more by drawing analogies from that company's eponym, the world's biggest and most complex rainforest. Scientists who study natural systems like the Amazon argue that they operate in a fundamentally different way than even a complicated machine. In a machine, like a car or an aircraft carrier, one can add up the parts to make a whole, understand in direct terms how one component of the machine interacts with others, and have reasonable confidence that once the machine gets running in a particular way, it will continue to operate in that way. Not so with natural systems. They are nonadditive and nonlinear, and they morph themselves continuously. That is why they are technically called "complex adaptive systems." For simplicity, I will refer to the US economy as a "natural system." Let's look at how the economy exhibits the three just-mentioned properties.

Natural systems are not the sum of their parts

In a natural system, the outcome is the product of the dynamic interactions between and among the parts rather than a simple addition of the outputs of the parts. That is, one can't just add up the parts and produce the whole. In fact, it is often hard to identify what the parts actually are. A family is a system. It is not possible to add up the individual features of a family and predict its functioning, because the interactions make it too hard to understand in advance how they will play out. The body is a system. One can't really divorce the functioning of the liver from that of the kidneys or the heart or even the brain, though modern approaches to medicine often attempt to do just that.

If the economy is a system like a family or the human body rather than a machine, that suggests that an approach based on managing the parts separately and simply adding their outputs—as Wassily Leontief and Otto Eckstein would have us do—will very likely result in a major dysfunction at some point.

That's precisely what we have seen happen with the economy. In the period between the end of the dot.com crash and recession, in 2002, and the beginning of the global financial crisis in 2008, the US Federal Reserve Board followed a policy of keeping interest rates unusually low in order to promote economic growth to make sure that America continued a strong recovery out of the recession. Meanwhile, the US government's two vehicles for promoting American home ownership, Fannie Mae and Freddie

Mac, were aggressively pursuing their assigned goals by securitizing bundles of mortgages so that banks could get those mortgages off their balance sheets and have greater capacity to make more mortgage loans.

Each policy made lots of sense on its own—promoting a stimulated economy and the expansion of American home ownership. But put together, they added up to something quite problematic. The low interest rates spurred a housing bubble, which burst, driving Fannie and Freddie into near insolvency requiring gigantic government bailouts while also contributing to the onset of the global financial crisis. If the economy really were like a machine, in which any given subsystem operates independently and does not influence any other subsystem, we would probably have been protected from this downside.

In natural systems, the relationships between inputs and outputs are nonlinear

It is challenging to follow the causal flows within natural systems and impossible to predict their overall effects. In the relationships among family members, more attention or monetary inputs do not produce more affection in some predictable, forecastable, linear way. They don't have zero impact, just not a linear or predictable one.

This idea was captured in the fanciful title of a 1972 speech by one of the pioneers of chaos theory, mathematician Edward Lorenz: "Predictability: Does the Flap of a Butterfly's Wings in Brazil Set Off a Tornado in Texas?" Following his speech, this idea became known as "the butterfly effect," which is meant to signify how the causal relationships between factors in a system can be entirely mysterious and nonlinear. Ever since, chaos and complexity theorists have been studying ways to better understand the nonlinear workings of natural systems.

The inability of economists to forecast complex economic systems suggests strongly that the economy's input–output relationships are nonlinear. Let's go back to the 2008 US forecasting debacle I described earlier. Forecasting skeptics Prakash Loungani and Hites Ahir extended the analysis of the US Blue Chip forecasts to worldwide forecasts, which were published in a report called Consensus Forecasts, covering dozens of countries. Of the seventy-seven countries included in the forecasts, forty-nine (64 percent) were in recession in 2009. However, as of September 2008, not one of those forty-nine countries was forecast to be in recession mere months later, in 2009.[4] It's unreasonable to infer that the highly trained, experienced economists making the forecasts were stupid or lazy, in which case we have to assume that what they were attempting to forecast was simply not forecastable using modeling approaches that assume linear or at least reasonably discernible input–output relationships.

Natural systems continuously adapt

In a natural system, all the participants attempt to optimize the outputs for their own benefit. If a child learns that in the current family system, bad behavior garners more attention, he may increase bad behavior to garner more attention even though the desire of the system is to produce less bad behavior. Participants don't even have to think consciously in order to adapt. Trees adapt to patterns of sunlight and weather. Where climate, for example, changes in a particular place, the wildlife and plants either adapt to the new conditions, move away, or are eventually outcompeted by better-adapted species.

The adaptations can be very specific to a context. The killer whales of Argentina's Valdes Peninsula, for example, have developed an extraordinary way of hunting for sea lions and seals that requires the whales to beach themselves. Whales will not ordinarily choose to do this. But the smooth pebbles of this particular stretch of beach allow the whales to work their way back into deeper water with the help of the surf. So they swim hard up on to the pebble beach to catch a seal that believes it is safe because it is on the beach—which normally it would be.[5] Notice also that what the whales are adapting to is the kind of environmental difference that could be quite difficult for even the actors themselves to realize. The whales here don't know that it's the pebbles they're reacting to—just that this hunting method works on this beach.

In the economy, we see the same process of adaptation. Economic agents behave in ways that they believe will increase their individual share of the economy's output. If the operating environment changes, people change what they do to reflect that. But behavioral adaptation is especially difficult to predict in social systems such as the economy—and we very often find that individually rational behaviors have a dysfunctional effect on the system as a whole.[6] For instance, companies routinely offer their salespeople financial incentives for meeting sales goals, in the belief that this will get them out selling. Instead, the salespeople spend huge amounts of time negotiating lower sales goals, because the payoff from negotiating a very makeable sales goal is higher than the payoff from working very hard to sell against a high but easily missed goal. The result of what is from the agent's perspective a very rational adaptation to the sales incentive is that the hundreds of millions of person-hours per year that could be spent on selling to customers are instead spent on negotiating targets.[7]

All three properties of natural systems are evident in the way financial markets and other parts of the economy work, and the comparison of the economy to a natural system is therefore certainly more valid than the machine analogy. But, as with any analogy, the comparison to nature must be made carefully, because not all natural systems are alike—and one important property that varies across systems is their stability.

In many natural systems, even highly complex ones, the relationships between input and output, and by extension their interrelationships, are fairly stable. This is true of rain forests and tundra, for example. Absent major external changes, such as a global-warming event, the evolution of these systems is slow and incremental. But other natural systems, such as the weather, are far more volatile. This is particularly true of natural systems that are predominantly social rather than biological. In social systems, like the economy, inputs are converted into outputs through adaptive behavior, and the relationships between those inputs and outputs become highly nonlinear and unstable because the behavior of intelligent agents is highly sensitive to any changes in the environment.

The economy, then, can best be viewed as a rapidly evolving and potentially unstable natural social system, in which intelligent players transact for their personal gain according to rules and processes that they design to facilitate those transactions—through laws, regulations, and the application of technologies. This creates the possibility that adaptive behavior turns into gaming, as individuals transact in the system in ways that suit their own immediate ends but subvert the system as a whole. And as we'll see in the pages that follow, the smart people always figure out how to game the system and any attempts we make to change the rules in order to prevent the small number of smart players from walking off with all the rewards are doomed to end in failure.

It Was Legal at Lehman

In 2002, Congress passed the Sarbanes–Oxley Act, colloquially called SOX, which was designed to put an end to the kind of murky dealings that had caused the collapses of Enron and World-Com. It didn't work. Capital-market insiders were absolutely un-daunted by the transparency that SOX had supposedly brought to the capital markets. They simply figured out new ways to work around the rules to their advantage, and this gaming, in fact, con-tributed to the severity of the 2008–2009 financial crisis. And no institution was more emblematic of this than investment bank Lehman Brothers.

As we now know, in the months leading up to its catastrophic crash and bankruptcy filing, on September 15, 2008, Lehman Brothers had been getting into ever deeper financial distress. Yet at no point did its quarterly financial statements, supposedly made clearer and more transparent by SOX, reflect Lehman's problems, because Lehman was still able to camouflage its decline by using sale-repurchase agreements to finance its operations, specifically the now infamous "Repo 105" vehicle. Repo 105 was and still is a legitimate accounting technique that allows a firm to classify a short-term loan as a sale.[8]

It worked like this: Just before the end of a quarter, Lehman would sell a large number of bonds (as much as $50 billion worth in the second quarter of 2008) that it undertook to repurchase a week or two later, after the end of the quarter. This gave Lehman the use of the money from the sale until the repurchase date, so the operation amounted to a secured loan. But Lehman could classify the money raised as a sale and use the proceeds to temporarily pay down its debt ahead of a reporting period. So, its balance sheet would look just fine unless one scrutinized the footnotes very carefully.[9]

After the quarterly statements were released, blessed by Leh-man's prestigious audit and legal advisors, Lehman would repay the short-term loan and reinflate its long-term debt. The public remained largely unaware of Lehman's true indebtedness and the methods the company was using to stay afloat in the short run.

This was all perfectly legal—Lehman scrupulously followed the letter of the law regarding Repo 105.[10]

Egregious as it was, what Lehman did in its efforts to stay in business seems almost benign in effect when you compare it with another, subtler, but arguably more subversive information game that's played out nearly every day in the supposedly level playing fields of the capital markets.

And the Band Plays On . . .

The stock markets essentially process information, which is then reflected in a company's stock price. The basic flow of that information goes like this: CEOs provide quarterly guidance on their companies' forthcoming results, and analysts create estimates based on that guidance and engage in the theater of holding the CEOs accountable for hitting their estimates. The investors, meanwhile, base their decisions on what CEOs say, how analysts interpret what CEOs say, and the consequent dialogue between the two.

The process in its current form dates back to 1983, when serial financial-market entrepreneur Jeffrey Parker created First Call, which aggregated analysts' forecasts into a "consensus estimate"—reducing all the analysis to a single, easily understood, widely disseminated number. It was an immediate hit for investors, because it gave a proxy for expected performance that reduced uncertainty about the future, and, after Parker sold the business to Thomson, First Call quickly established itself as a key component of the market infrastructure.

At first, in order to protect investors, regulations limited the information that the CEO could share, and speculation by CEOs about the future was discouraged. Consequently, the analysis focused largely on interpreting historical numbers and the potential consequences of actual decisions already made. But then, in 1995, Congress passed the Private Securities Litigation Reform Act. This act facilitated the making of "forward-looking statements" by CEOs. All a CEO had to do was note that the information was being shared under the "safe harbor" provision, which warned investors that the CEO was speculating about the future. Protected by the safe harbor, CEOs began to spend a lot of time and energy on providing guidance.

This has been producing some interesting results. Before 1995, US publicly traded companies beat their consensus estimates 50 percent of the time, as one would expect given the uncertain nature of economic activities. But by 1997, just two years after the passage of the Reform Act, the very same companies were meeting or beating their consensus estimates an impressive 70 percent of the time.[11]

The most likely interpretation on this change in performance relative to the consensus estimate is that like salesmen negotiating their targets, CEOs had started to exploit the safe-harbor provision in order to influence or manage investors' and analysts' expectations down to a level the CEOs could easily beat.[12] The late Jack Welch was a notable example. During the heart of his tenure as General Electric's CEO, the company met or beat analysts' forecasts in forty-six of forty-eight quarters between December 31, 1989, and September 30, 2001—a 96 percent hit rate. Even more impressively, in forty-one of those forty-six quarters, GE hit the analysts' forecast to the exact penny—89 percent perfection—and in the remaining seven imperfect quarters, the tolerance was startlingly narrow: GE beat the projection by 2 cents four times and by 1 cent once, and it missed by 1 cent once and by 2 cents once. The chance of all of that happening randomly is infinitesimal.[13] This kind of expectations management could be highly lucrative for the CEOs involved, because CEO compensation is almost always heavily influenced by stock-price movements. And regardless of the absolute level of performance, a stock nearly always performs better if the company meets or beats analyst earnings expectations.

Note that none of these information games actually results in the creation of any real value. The stock-price effects produced by managing expectations will introduce only temporary improvements in the share price. The price will eventually correct, as real information comes in, and the net effect of the gaming I've been describing will simply be to introduce more volatility into the share price. The only beneficiaries of this will be the CEOs managing the expectations (possibly around their option vesting dates) and investment institutions such as hedge funds that make their gains on identifying arbitrage opportunities in highly volatile markets. The volatility offers no benefit to long-term investors such as pension funds and insurance companies and arguably imposes costs on the very companies that the market was created to support—new enterprises seeking capital to finance economic growth.

. . . And Faster

It's not just about the rules. Technology also creates opportunities for gaming that ultimately subvert the system. Back in 2011, the New York Stock Exchange (NYSE), by far the country's most important stock exchange, opened a new outpost in Mahwah, New Jersey, a bucolic township of twenty-five thousand inhabitants about an hour's drive north of Wall Street. One reason for creating the facility was pretty standard. Trading-technology infrastructure takes up a lot of space, so moving it from expensive Manhattan to low-cost Mahwah saved money for the exchange.

But another reason for the move was more novel. The NYSE built the facility big enough to lease out space to third parties, enabling it to derive new revenue in addition to the cost savings. But who on earth would want to lease space in an NYSE facility in rural New Jersey? Turns out, finding takers wasn't a problem. In fact, trading firms were very eager for the opportunity. These firms understood that having their servers in close proximity to NYSE servers would create a speed advantage. It would mean that trades from their colocated servers would reach the NYSE servers a few milliseconds faster than trades from servers not in the facility. This might sound like no difference at all, but the firms in question engage in what's known as high-speed trading, in which a computer makes buy and sell decisions based on miniscule arbitrage opportunities in market prices, and shares are often held for fractions of a second. For this type of trading, getting your order to the front of the trading queue is not the most important thing—it is the only thing.

It was a nice moneymaker for the NYSE, because the rents at its facility are steep by rural New Jersey standards. But the NYSE immediately had a challenge: how would it allocate space within the facility? Some server bays were closer to the NYSE server and therefore had fractional time advantages over those that were farther away. Should the exchange auction off the real estate by location? Should the bay immediately beside the NYSE server cost five times the bay near the back door? Or should it be ten times? Any tiered pricing approach was likely to create an arms race within the building, which would be unseemly. The clever folks at the NYSE came up with a better solution. Regardless of where lessees were located within the facility, their servers would be connected to the NYSE servers with cables of equal length. There would be no arms race within their facility.[14] Of course, the arms race will certainly continue elsewhere, and the solution does no favors to traders who are not engaged in high-frequency trading but who simply wish to transact trades on behalf of clients. Since trading stocks is a zero-sum game, whatever extra the high-frequency traders make with their techniques comes out of the pockets of normal traders, including pension funds and traditional money managers.

This example illustrates several points about gaming the market and its effects. To begin with, it shows how quick players in the financial markets are at exploiting changes in the rules, regulations, and infrastructures surrounding the markets. It also shows that as the markets become more complex and technologically enabled, the cumulative small advantages that come from high-frequency trading are creating more and more of a gap between those players with the capital and know-how to engage in high-speed trading and those without. Spread Networks, for example, invested hundreds of millions of dollars to build a fiber-optic link along the shortest route between the NYSE and the Chicago Board of Trade. The link cut transmission time to an estimated 13.3 milliseconds. But that is a proverbial slow boat to China compared with the two microwave networks under construction, which promise to cut the time down to 8 to 9 milliseconds, because microwave is more direct than fiber-optical cable.[15]

As all these clever adaptations and the ensuing adaptations to the adaptations take place, we gradually see the stock market losing sight of its original purpose, which was to help companies issue stock to the public in order to enable the companies to grow their businesses. In doing so, the stock market also enabled investors to participate in and benefit from the growth of the companies in which they invested. The creation of the Securities and Exchange Commission, in 1934, attempted to make sure traders didn't supersede issuers or investors in the pecking order. But, with high-speed trading now accounting for as much as 70 percent of trading on the NYSE, it's hardly surprising if we see the NYSE traders first, investors second, and issuers last—a completely upside-down world.[16] Did the NYSE have issuers or investors in mind when it set up its operation in Mahwah? No, it was all about the traders.

And the traders do very well for themselves. Even a small technology advantage in trading today can translate into billions of dollars in profits. That's why almost 10 percent (thirty-one) of the 2019 *Forbes* 400 list of the richest Americans got on the list by trading stocks as principals of hedge funds, charging their investors (most typically) 2 percent per year of assets under management plus 20 percent of any upside created.[17] Meanwhile, a quick review of the issuers, America's public companies, will reveal that there are getting to be fewer and fewer of them, as it has become ever more onerous for a company to choose the public markets as the venue for raising capital. The private markets are much more friendly and conducive to growth. Between 1997 and 2015, the number of public companies in the US fell by half (from 7,507 to 3,766), while private-equity investment skyrocketed.[18]

The Gamer's Paradise

Both the democratic and the capitalist parts of American society offer rich pickings for gamers. The 2018 federal budget, for example, stood at $4.4 trillion. It is no surprise, then, to see the billions of dollars ($3.42 billion in 2018) invested officially each year by the more than ten thousand registered lobbyists in Washington increasing by 60 percent in real terms over the past twenty years, despite many measures to stop lobbying.[19] And nobody knows how much additional unofficial money is spent to influence that $4.4 trillion game. Then there was the $6.5 billion spent on the presidential and Congressional elections in 2016, investments in gaining favor with those most central to gaming the Washington game.

It is difficult to measure the true size of the stock-market game by the same metric as that of the US budget. But the annual turnover of stocks in US stock markets amounted to $33 trillion in

2018.[20] One can quickly see why the industry reacts with terror to any proposal to impose a "Tobin tax" on trading. The idea of such a tax dates back to 1972, when Nobel Laureate James Tobin proposed the imposition of a currency-trading tax in order to limit the economically destabilizing effects of currency volatility. Tobin's initial suggestion was for a rate of 0.5 percent on the value of the transaction, which, if applied to stock trades, would—on the current trading level—yield almost $200 billion per year in taxes, though the complex adaptive system would surely adjust quickly to find ways around the tax. Another way to measure the magnitude of the US stock markets is by the market capitalization of the companies listed, which for the biggest exchange, the New York Stock Exchange, is about $29 trillion.[21] It is no wonder that tens of thousands of financial engineers work in trading departments across Wall Street and beyond, figuring out how to game stock markets for their narrow benefit.

In addition to the size of the prize, gamers are attracted by the duration of the payoffs: that is, the number of years the gaming effort will be effective before the system adapts again to eliminate it. The longer this period, the more likely it is that gamers will invest in gaming. Such, in fact, is the case for both the US government and the US stock markets. The two political parties fight hard to put through legislation and are opposed as vigorously as possible to each other's efforts in that vein, because once legislation is in place, it is hard to change. Think about the Affordable Care Act—aka Obamacare. For six years after its passage, the Republican party ran against Obamacare, promising to "repeal and replace." Despite achieving the triple win of the presidency, the Senate, and the House in the 2016 election, the Republican party was incapable of either repealing or replacing Obamacare. All gamers who invested in making profits off of Obamacare will have decades to ply their profitable trade.

Similarly, it takes years for stock-market operations or regulations to change, even after it is clear that the system is being gamed, partly because the hugely wealthy gamers often end up capturing the exchanges, as we saw with the NYSE and its Mahwah trading operation. "Market specialists" whose job it is to ensure that there are relatively fluid markets in each stock on an exchange have been making supernormal returns year after year after year without stock exchanges doing a thing to stop that game. In this environment, gamers can feel confident in making multibillion-dollar investments in order to get their orders to the NYSE servers faster than the next trader—confident that this gaming of the system will earn them a handsome return on their investment.

Finally, while the yearly size of the prize may be big and the likely duration long, if the probability of successfully gaming the system in question appears low, potential gamers won't invest. If, on the other hand, the gaming has a clear success model with a high probability of success, investment will be huge. Laws that pass the US Congress are supposed to be unbiased and in the interests of the American electorate overall. If that were in fact the case, it would be hard to explain the spending of $3.42 billion on lobbying in one year by more narrowly interested parties. Those spenders are motivated by the strong probability of success for their gaming efforts—and are investing in a big game.

When it comes to probability of success, upward and downward spirals take shape quickly. If a system shows itself susceptible to gaming, more gaming investments will be made, because the heightened expectation of success makes those investments more attractive. If early gaming efforts fail, the assumed probability of success falls, curtailing gaming investments. This is the reason why, historically, the island nations of Singapore and Hong Kong have worked hard to gain reputations for low probabilities of gaming success in their jurisdictions in comparison with the jurisdictions around them. Spending there to influence govern-ment policy decisions has been considered a poor investment, be-cause the probability of payoff is just too low.

The economy and US politics are just the two biggest markets for gaming in the US system of democratic capitalism. There are countless others that exhibit self-interested adaptive behaviors like those I've been describing. Those behaviors are only encouraged by our adoption of the machine as a metaphor for the economy. That metaphor causes us to defend our "improvements," which makes the gaming ever more lucrative because it extends the life of the gaming opportunities the new rules may create. When even-tually the "improvements" are discredited, new rules are brought in, triggering a new round of adapted behaviors, and the gaming cycle continues. The result is an increasingly upside-down world, in which a privileged few benefit in the short term while the long-term interests of the many are sacrificed.

We have no choice but to reject the machine metaphor and to recognize that America's democratic capitalism is more akin to a natural system—one that is complex and adaptive. As such, it needs to be managed in a completely different fashion, because applying approaches that work for a machine will undermine an already fairly unstable system's resilience by giving more scope for people to game the system more successfully and for longer. The current outcomes are neither a coincidence nor an aberration. They are to be expected and, if anything, are a precursor of a more extreme future.

So, what should we be doing instead? The next chapter turns to the design principles that should underlie how we manage our complex adaptive system, and which will set the stage for the prac-tical advice to follow for the stakeholders in our system, who both transact in the system and drive its evolution: business executives, political leaders, educators, and citizens.

Part Two

SOLUTIONS

Chapter 5

Achieving Balance in America's Natural System

Toy lovers woke up September 19, 2017, to the shocking news that Toys "R" Us had filed for bankruptcy the previous day. Six months later, over twenty million radio listeners were similarly shocked when they learned that iHeartMedia, the owner of their favorite radio station, also filed for bankruptcy. We typically assume that bankruptcy is what happens to badly managed companies. But it is something of a stretch to think of America's number-one toy retailer and its biggest radio-station operator as bad companies. Industry leaders are not usually badly managed.

What got those companies into trouble was not a failure to win customers. It was, quite simply, that both companies were owned by leveraged-buyout (LBO) firms, whose business model involves purchasing companies that appear to have a robust cash flow and then leveraging up their capital structures to replace expensive equity with cheap debt.[1] As a result Toys "R" Us was "saddled with debt" and iHeartMedia was put under a "crushing load of debt," according to close observers.[2] So, although the companies were reasonably well-managed from an operational perspective, the massive debt loads they were forced to carry had increased the risks of defaulting should overall industry conditions deteriorate, and these were indeed tricky times in retailing and media. The LBO firms that purchased Toys "R" Us and iHeartMedia learned the hard way that greater apparent capital efficiency is not necessarily better, and their investments had to be written off.

Imposing debt on the scale that Toys "R" Us and iHeartMedia were required to carry is predicated on the ability of the LBO firms to predict those companies' future cash flows fairly precisely. The belief that a high degree of precision is possible is itself rooted in a model in which companies operate as cogs in a machine. But as we have seen, the economy is not a machine in which the players are cogs. Businesses are part of a natural and highly complex system, characterized by a large number of interdependencies and contingencies, which makes estimating their future cash flows with anything resembling precision a fool's errand. The systems are adaptive in that players inside the company modify their behavior to take into account the fact that the company is now operated with one goal in mind: maximizing the benefit to the LBO-firm investors, with no regard whatsoever for employees. What's more, changes in parts of the system have ramifications outside those parts—cutting staff and capital investments translates into lower investments in customer satisfaction, which increases the risks to revenues.

The bottom line is that a relentless and unconstrained drive for capital efficiency saps LBO acquisitions of all of their resilience. Equity providers are not owed any fixed payment in any given year. So, if a firm does badly in the trough of a market, it doesn't have to pay a dividend (or any other form of payment) to the equity holders. In contrast, debt payments must be made regardless of the performance of the firm. Any homeowner knows the story. It is never a pleasant thing to lose your job. But if your mortgage has been paid off, the experience is not likely to be financially catastrophic. However, if your house is mortgaged to the hilt, you will probably lose it and perhaps more. In similar fashion, having a relatively high proportion of equity in its capital structure increases a company's resilience to downturns (like having a paid-off house and therefore no monthly mortgage payment). The LBO firms destroyed the resilience provided by having a buffer of equity, in order to achieve a financially efficient capital structure, and that is what sank Toys "R" Us and iHeartMedia. Their businesses weren't bad, but their financial structures certainly were.

The core design challenge for the future of American democratic capitalism is to achieve a much better balance between efficiency and resilience in the system than exhibited by these LBO disasters. It is a delicate balance, as there is danger on both sides. Pursuit of all resilience and no efficiency is as problematic as pursuit of efficiency with no resilience. The only difference is in the nature of the death.

Nonresilient systems tend to die explosively. The US capital markets blew up spectacularly in 2008–2009, and could well have gone extinct had it not been for intervention by the US government. In 2011, in Japan's Fukushima nuclear-reactor disaster, two of the reactors, lacking resilient systems, melted down and then the buildings housing them exploded, spewing massive levels of radiation into the region. To be sure, the tsunami that caused the catastrophe was a low-probability event. But the downside to that weak resilience has been and will continue to be tremendous. The latest estimate of the cleanup costs alone is over $600 billion, and that doesn't include the costs of having a still-uninhabitable zone around the plant, with citizens perhaps permanently displaced.[3]

In contrast, inefficient systems tend to fade away slowly, as systems with superior fitness replace them. There is no way to guarantee the resilience of a system that doesn't pay attention to efficiency. It may appear to be resilient, but it will eventually be overwhelmed by a more efficient adversary. The authorities could have wrapped the Fukushima nuclear facility in layer upon layer of redundancy to make it particularly resilient. But the cost would likely have been so high that it would have made the power produced economically unviable.

So, what does the pursuit of that delicate balance involve in the context of democratic capitalism? Recall that in the economic context, more and more efficiency converts a Gaussian distribution of outcomes into a Pareto one, as the more efficient agents take a larger proportion of economic value. Since prior outcomes influence future outcomes in the economic context, the slide toward Pareto is accentuated, amplifying the direct efficiency effects. To correct for this imbalance, we need to explicitly retire the machine model of the economy and consciously adopt the model of the natural system. Hence, our design principles for achieving the delicate but more desirable balance have to take account of the three core features of a natural system: its complexity, its adaptivity, and its systemic structure. While doing so, we must not forget that we are modeling and that whenever we model, we risk letting the proxies for progress surrogate themselves for the model itself. Hence, we need to be more conscious both about how we model our complex adaptive system and about how we measure its progress.

Design for Complexity

The key challenge of complexity is that the operation of a complex system is so opaque and inscrutable that it is not feasible to predict performance with even reasonable accuracy, as illustrated earlier by economists' forecasts of both America's 2008–2009 economic performance and the consequences (or lack thereof) of the "fiscal cliff." This means that forecasting just how much pressure a system can bear and then applying that exact amount of pressure is a more dangerous game than we imagine. LBO firms tend to think that having a high debt load—and hence high annual interest payments—puts productive pressure on management to perform. Tell that to the management teams of Toys "R" Us and iHeartMedia. Or tell the managers at Wells Fargo who faced extreme pressure to have their customers open more accounts that the pressure was actually good for them. While pressure can produce more efficiency, when applied without constraints, it produces Pareto results—and worse.

The design principle, therefore, is to balance *pressure* for more efficiency with *friction* to limit its damaging extremes. This will involve taking actions and establishing rules and practices that moderate and limit the amount of pressure that can be applied to a system, in order to protect against results that are both unpredictable and negative or even catastrophic in their consequences. This, I must emphasize, is not a radical or new concept. The voluntary imposition of limits and constraints in the interest of prolonging the lifespan of a system or economic agent is a survival strategy as old as humanity itself. Let me illustrate the deliberate introduction of friction in the context of America's most iconic sport: baseball.

Mel Stottlemyre was a beloved and successful New York Yankees pitcher in the 1960s and 1970s. He won 164 games (214th all-time in major-league history) over his eleven-year career and was named an All-Star in five of those eleven seasons. He had two baseball-playing sons, Mel Jr. and Todd. Both were considered truly elite prospects as young, minor-league pitchers. However, Mel Jr. pitched only a small portion of one year in the major leagues, accumulating zero career wins, while his younger brother Todd pitched for fifteen years, won 136 games, and pitched for two World Series Champion teams. The only real difference between the brothers? Mel Jr. blew out his arm (torn rotator cuff, for baseball aficionados) while still in the minor leagues and Todd didn't.

Baseball pitchers live in constant danger of overstressing their pitching arm to the point of career-ending injury. And in the complexity of elite pitching, it is hard to figure out when it might happen and, when it does, why. Clearly, some of it is genetic and some is random. But one factor that has come into focus in the time since Mel Jr. blew out his arm is the number of pitches a starting pitcher throws in a given game. It is not the first 80 pitches of the game that are likely to overstress a pitcher's arm: it is the last 30 pitches in a 110-pitch game. But an aggressive pitcher will likely feel he can pitch forever—and an aggressive coach will be very tempted to believe him, especially in a crunch game. And that is precisely why in modern baseball, there are pitch-count restrictions (and innings-per-year restrictions) imposed on pitchers by their teams, especially with respect to young pitchers.[4]

These restrictions arguably hurt efficiency. Other things being equal, the team would want its best pitcher to pitch more innings of more games. And for a while, that might pay off. But with each game the risks will rise that the pitcher's arm will be overstressed, forcing the pitcher to bow out for a protracted period—if not forever. Pitch-count restrictions are a guard against that—they make it more likely that the pitcher will be able to bounce back from each pitching start and will perform well for the entire year, and the next, and the next. I find it useful to think about pitch-count restrictions as a productive friction. By limiting the use of a particular resource or system component (the pitcher), the life and usefulness of that resource are prolonged, to the overall benefit of the system.

Similar friction is imposed in NASCAR stock-car racing. On the fastest, highest-banked tracks, the cars are mandated to use "restrictor plates" that reduce the airflow between the carburetor and the intake manifold and thus bring down the maximum speed of the car, because the highest speeds are too dangerous for those tracks. The plates serve as a constraint on the inherent efficiency of the engine. Drivers don't love them. But they save lives.[5]

The balance of pressure with friction is not limited to the world of sports. The US Federal Reserve Board, for example, uses interest rates as its "restrictor plate." If the Fed feels that the economy is heating up too much and in danger of creating an economic bubble and/or inflation, it can use monetary tightening to push interest rates higher—creating friction intended to slow growth. The previously mentioned Tobin tax on currency trading was explicitly viewed as an imposed friction that would slow down the most dramatic and damaging swings in currency movements. By adding a cost to the execution of each trade, currency traders would be discouraged from trading in an unfettered way that would drive down the currency of a given country.

Of course, the principle isn't to eliminate the pressure for efficiency. That would be equally disastrous. The principle is to create friction that ameliorates the damaging extremes of pressure—that is, by avoiding those times when more pressure is not better.

Design for Adaptivity

As we have seen above, the complexity aspect of a complex adaptive system means that the system in question is largely inscrutable, with causal relationships among elements in the system that are ambiguous and nonlinear. Even more challenging, those relationships aren't stable. The actors in the system are continuously driving adaptation of the system. By the time we decide what to do, it is quite possible, if not likely, that the system has changed in a way that renders our decision obsolete by the time it is acted upon. And by the time we have figured that out, the system will have changed again. Because of that adaptability, our design principle must be to balance the desire for *perfection* with the drive for *improvement*.

In a machine model, the pursuit of perfection makes sense. It is sensible to analyze the machine in every detail in order to understand how to maximize its performance and, once that optimum performance level has been achieved, then defend against any attempt to change the way the machine works—because it is performing as well as it possibly can. At this point, any failure in the machine's performance is likely to be interpreted as pilot error or not giving the machine enough input or time. This is what philosophers call a justificationist stance. There is a perfect answer out there to be sought, and when that perfect answer is found, the search is over. The task then turns from searching for the perfect answer to protecting the perfect answer against any attempt to alter it. It feels noble to aim for, fight for, and protect perfection.

However, in an adaptive system, there is no perfect destination; there is no end to the journey. The actors in it keep adapting to how it works. In nature, this happens reflexively, as with a tree that turns to the sunlight due to the force of nature, and by growing taller obscures the sunlight for those in its increasing shadow. In the economy, adaptation happens reflectively. People take in the available inputs and make choices, and those choices influence the choices and behaviors of the other humans in the system. This means that players will try to game any change in a system the moment that change is put in place. It is both natural and inevitable. If you are offered a bonus for achieving your sales budget, you will work hardest not to sell more of the product or service in question but rather to negotiate the lowest possible sales budget to make achieving it easiest and most likely. If you are the Lehman Brothers CEO and CFO and you know that investors will punish you if you report a high level of debt, then you will use the Repo 105 device in ways that were never intended, in order to disguise your dangerously excessive level of debt. Attempting to prevent gaming with an inspired design is therefore a fool's errand. Gamers will exploit whatever solution is in place, and sooner or later the solution will become dysfunctional.

So, although the pursuit of perfection may seem like a noble goal, in a complex adaptive system it is delusional and dangerous. In a cruel paradox, seeking perfection does not enhance the probability of achieving said perfection. In a complex adaptive system, it is not possible to know in advance the organized, sequential steps toward perfection. Guesses can be made. Better and worse vectors can be reasonably chosen. But perfection is an unrealistic direct goal, with the problematic downside of creating a paradise for gamers. As justificationists staunchly defend a system they perceive to be perfect, gamers are only given more time and space to enrich themselves at the system's long-term expense.

Hence, we must balance the understandable desire for perfection with an incessant drive for improvement. Given the impossibility of finding anything resembling a permanent fix, we need to engage the system not in a spirit of periodically and dramatically fixing it, despite the political attractiveness of seeming to offer "the answer," but rather with the intention of tweaking it on a continuous, incremental basis. Those tweaks will never be perfect. In a complex adaptive system, there are no perfect answers, or even perfect directions. There are just better and worse ones in the moment. And the best ones will still be found wanting. Error is not a bug: it is a feature, an important and inevitable signal that it is time to initiate another intervention into the complex adaptive system. The experience of error is consistent with the march toward ever-better answers—ever-better models. Even the cleverest designs will be gamed. Like the economy, software works as a natural system in this respect as well: hackers will always hack, and patches will always be needed—again and again and again.

The approach of continuously tweaking rather than seeking singular perfection should resonate with the American legal community. America's common-law legal system (borrowed, of course, from England), in contrast to the civil-law systems found in France, Germany, Japan, and China, for example, is based on the principle that the laws of the land will be tweaked through their interpretation by judges in the context of specific cases. American democratic capitalism should take a page from American jurisprudence in embracing relentless tweaking as the best way to progress toward a perfection that will never be achieved.[6]

Design for Systemic Structure

Recall that in a natural system there are numerous interdependencies among the elements in the system. The core design principle with respect to the systemic structure is to balance *connectedness* with *separation*. As with the overall balance between efficiency and resilience, and with complexity balance between pressure and friction, and adaptivity balance between perfection and improvement, there is danger on both sides of the desirable path.

With respect to connectedness, as we've seen, interdependence between outcomes over time amplifies the gravity effect of efficiency. It's no surprise, therefore, that the transformation from a Gaussian distribution to a Pareto distribution is accelerating. We are currently connecting more and more things, in more and more tightly coupled ways.[7] The internet of things (IoT) is the latest generation of enhanced connectedness. Untold billions of devices will be connected to provide real-time information, computer-to-computer. Systems everywhere are becoming tightly coupled. Lots about it is good, indeed very good. A connected world is more efficient. A connected world drives out transaction costs and unnecessary rework. Humans are already tightly connected at fractional costs; now machines will be too, and machines to humans, and vice versa.

But tightly coupled systems can fail catastrophically. In 2003, the entire US Northeast (plus Central Canada) experienced a power blackout because a single power line in Ohio came in contact with a tree branch. This relatively minor fault cascaded through the tightly coupled system and, once it hit a critical stage, 265 power plants went off-line in about three minutes. It took a week to put that particular Humpty-Dumpty back together, during which tens of millions of people and their businesses went without electrical power.[8]

The solution for avoiding this sort of calamity is not full separation. It is to attempt to understand and benefit from connectedness but balance it with separation, because when outcomes are interdependent, effects become the causes of more of the given effect and the proverbial sand pile collapses. That is precisely why tightly coupled systems are prone to total meltdowns. The most direct way to reduce dysfunctional connectedness is to install firebreaks, an idea that comes from forest management. In a dry season, a bolt of lightning may set a tree ablaze, and if there is a strong wind and all the trees are dry, the fire can spiral rapidly out of control. To reduce the risk of losing commercial timber to fire, forest managers introduce gaps across which the fires cannot easily pass, whether that is an existing road or a stream or a path that is bulldozed to impede a forest fire already underway. It creates productive separation in a system that is too tightly coupled to exhibit the requisite resilience.

Productive separation has long been a tool in financial regulation. The Glass–Steagall Act of 1933, which was part of the New Deal legislative agenda, was designed to create a firebreak between the banking and securities industries after the crash of 1929. To be sure, some historians do not believe that the crash of 1929 was driven by commercial banks inappropriately participating excessively in the securities business, but that was certainly the assumption of the framers of Glass–Steagall, which prevented commercial and investment banking institutions from venturing into each other's businesses. The idea was that if one of the industries experienced a meltdown, the other would remain relatively unaffected. In 1956, the Bank Holding Company Act plowed a further firebreak, between banking and insurance.

These firebreaks were removed starting in the 1980s in the spirit of efficiency and connectedness. The theory was that a firm that spanned these industries would be able to serve customers in a broader and more seamless fashion and would therefore be a more efficient delivery mechanism. Once again, experts disagree on the consequences of the removal of this firebreak. Some view the removal as a factor contributing to the global financial crisis.[9] Others view it as not relevant. It is never possible to be certain in such a complex adaptive system, but it is clear that adaptation of a sort not necessarily anticipated by those removing the firebreaks ran rampant. The largest commercial banks in the country used retail deposits to fund risky securities-industry activities that would have horrified those depositors had they known what the capital base provided by their deposits was being used to underwrite.

Another bit of productive separation is the circuit-breaker system used today on most stock markets. The idea of the circuit breaker was spurred by the October 19, 1987, fall in the Dow Jones Industrial Average of 508 points. It was the biggest absolute (though not relative) drop in history. The problem was that the effect (dropping stock prices) became the cause (I should sell now before the market drops further) of more of the effect (dropping stock prices) and so on, for 508 points of decline.[10] The tight connection of instant data and instant reaction producing more data and more instant reactions had to be separated. That was achieved by way of a circuit breaker. Following a drop of predetermined magnitude, trading would be halted to give the participants a chance to think more carefully, so that they wouldn't simply react as fast as possible in order to get their trades in before others and not lose so much.

While there are examples of firebreaks designed to balance connectedness with separation, there simply aren't enough. Some, as in the case of Glass–Steagall, are being eliminated in pursuit of higher connectedness for efficiency. It might be justifiable in individual cases, because balance, not an extreme of separation, is the goal. However, the balance between higher connectedness for efficiency and greater separation for resilience needs at present to be redressed in favor of separation.

As you manage this balance, be aware that connectedness is an inherent property of natural systems and a source of efficiency, which needs encouragement as much as resilience needs protection. It is important to look out for and recognize these connections, because failing to recognize them means that you run the risk of a reductionist's trap: not recognizing when dysfunction in one part of the system may spread to another part. A further complication is that many important connections hide in plain sight.

To illustrate, let me take you down a connection that contributed to the collapse in the mortgage-backed bond market in 2008. In the capital-markets system, investors who buy bonds, including portfolios of derivatives based on bonds, count on bond-rating agencies—Standard & Poor's (S&P), Moody's, and Fitch—to help them judge the riskiness of the bonds in which they are investing. Some investors, like pension funds, are required to hold only bonds that are rated "investment grade" (above BBB– for S&P and Fitch or Baa3 for Moody's) in order to make sure that these funds are not taking risks that put in jeopardy the retirement payments owed to pensioners current and future. Hence, they *must* use the bond raters. Other investors *choose* to avail themselves of the reports of bond raters in order to manage their risks.

To do a useful job in rating bonds, bond raters at any one of these rating agencies need to be very talented and experienced at understanding with great precision the inherent risk associated with the entities issuing the bonds they are rating, and the degree to which the bond holder is or is not protected from those risks by the covenants in the bonds' debenture agreements.

The interesting thing about anybody who happens to be highly skilled at that core and necessary task is that they would also be great at trading bonds. And trading bonds—whether on one's own behalf or for a bond-trading company or the bond-trading desk of a larger financial institution—is far more lucrative than working as a bond rater for one of the three bond-rating agencies. Hence, while there will be inevitable exceptions to the rule, most people who happen to be very highly skilled at understanding bonds well enough to rate them will be sitting at a bond-trading desk, not a bond-rating desk. Ones that aren't so good at rating bonds will be occupying the majority of the desks at bond-rating agencies.

Observers and participants were surprised and outraged at how dreadful the bond-rating agencies had been at rating the packages of mortgage-backed bonds that triggered, or at the very least exacerbated, the global financial crisis. In our system for ensuring the stability of the capital markets, we assumed that bond-rating agencies were staffed by experts in rating bonds, who would consistently provide high-quality advice to bond investors. However, during the financial crisis, large volumes of mortgage-backed bonds rated AAA by the bond raters defaulted despite the reasonable expectation of investors that the default rate for AAA bonds is virtually nil. It should have been impossible for bundles of mortgages expertly rated AAA—metaphorical miles away from the marginal BBB– rating—to default and in some cases lose all their value. And yet they did, and in large volumes.

The fundamental problem was that the truly expert bond raters weren't rating bonds at S&P, Moody's, or Fitch. They were at bond funds and investment banks, busily creating structured bond portfolios designed to fool less savvy bond investors and their overmatched bond raters into believing that the structured bond products were AAA-grade when they were actually thinly disguised junk. Why did this happen? Fundamentally it is because the players involved in the system, from investors to regulators, assumed the absence of any connection between the system by which bond experts chose their place of employment and the system by which bond ratings of a given assumed quality are generated. In reality, those two systems were connected in a subtle but fundamental fashion, the ignorance of which created significant damage.

Designing to avoid this underappreciation of connectedness—i.e., too much assumed separation—is tricky. The complexity element of a complex adaptive system ensures that it is not a straightforward task to identify all the relationships in the system. Once again, systems-theorist professor John Sterman provides useful perspective: "There are no side effects—only effects. Those we thought of in advance, the ones we like, we call the main, or intended, effects, and take credit for them. The ones we didn't anticipate, the ones that came around and bit us in the rear—those are the 'side effects.'"[11]

It would be unhelpful to admonish designers to figure out all the effects in advance so that the system doesn't fail because of "side effects," since there will always be unexpected effects. On September 11, 2001, the majority of large organizations located in lower Manhattan had carefully designed backup telecommunications facilities to take over in case their primary one failed. However, none of those organizations anticipated that the majority of the redundant communications cables in lower Manhattan ran directly under the World Trade Center and would be wiped out because the Twin Towers collapsed.[12] To ask the designers to anticipate a terrorist attack that would destroy New York's two biggest buildings is entirely unrealistic.

But it is not unrealistic to ask designers of systems to pay close attention to unexpected effects when they show themselves, rather than ignore them because they don't fit the model. I learned an important lesson in this when I studied what helped Dr. Stephen Scherer become one of the world's preeminent researchers of autism spectrum disorder and genomics. For Scherer, anomalies are a treasure trove: "My belief is that answers to really difficult problems can often be found in the data points that don't seem to fit existing frameworks. To me, those little variations are like signposts saying: Don't ignore me!" He believes that all of his research successes stem from paying attention to "the data that everybody else was throwing away."[13]

While Dr. Scherer may be in the minority in terms of keeping an eagle eye on effects that don't comport with the model of the day, he isn't alone in doing so. Sometimes the financial regulators do pay attention. When the consensus estimates of analysts and their buy/hold/sell recommendations became more important and central to the capital markets in the wake of the creation of First Call and the passage of the Private Securities Litigation Reform Act, as described in chapter 4, regulators noticed that the analyst ratings were getting ever more dramatically weighted toward "buy" recommendations. Why would that be? Well it was very helpful to the analysts' colleagues in the investment-banking department, when attempting to sell business to a given company, if there was a positive, optimistic buy recommendation out on the stock of that company. While regulators had hoped that the analysts would do rigorous evaluation of each company's stock and provide an unbiased recommendation, it turned out that there was an unforeseen connection between the hopes and desires of the investment bankers and the preponderance of buy recommendations on the part of their analyst colleagues.

In 2002, in response to understanding this connection, the Securities and Exchange Commission imposed a rule called Financial Industry Regulatory Authority (FINRA) Rule 2711 mandating that "a member must disclose in each research report the percentage of all securities rated by the member to which the member would assign a 'buy,' 'hold/neutral,' or 'sell' rating."[14] While it is unlikely that this has fixed the problem entirely, at least it adjusts to connectedness where it was shown both to exist and to produce problematic outcomes.

In these ways, designing for systemic nature can create productive separation where tight coupling threatens to produce extreme Pareto outcomes and can adjust for nonobvious connectedness that would otherwise produce equally problematic outcomes.

Summary, and Introduction to the Agendas for Change

To summarize, the overall design principle for repairing the dysfunctions in our democratic capitalist system is to balance *efficiency* with *resilience*. To achieve that overall balance, we need to pursue three individual balances, first between the pursuit of *pressure* and the application of productive *friction*, second between the desire for *perfection* and the drive for *improvement*, and third between the march toward *connectedness* and the enforcement of *separation*. The prescriptions for a broken system need to be consistent with the nature of that system—in this case a complex adaptive system, not a complicated machine.

As we embark on our journey to repair our broken system, we need to recognize that no single actor can create the necessary shift on his or her own. Unsurprisingly, in this complex system, there are many important and interrelated actors. Given the diagnosis to date, it would be silly and unrealistic to imagine that one actor could fix the problems identified. All the stakeholders in democratic capitalism have their parts to play. Business executives need to embrace that they are participating in a complex adaptive system rather than operating a machine—and manage accordingly. Political leaders need to recognize both that their job is not to promote unalloyed pursuit of efficiency and that they are overseeing a complex adaptive system rather than a perfectible machine. Educators need to understand that their job is to prepare graduates to operate effectively in a complex adaptive system—and teach accordingly. Citizens have to take on the assignment of aiding the functioning of the complex adaptive system by enforcing more friction in order to encourage more resilience.

As mentioned earlier, in a break with tradition in books of this sort, I will recommend only prescriptions that have already been used or are in place. They may come from a different context or jurisdiction or time. But they are not theoretical; they are actual. They aren't speculative; they are doable. There are lots of them. We don't necessarily need all of them, but we need most of them together to restore balance and save American democratic capitalism.

That will have a particular implication for readers. A business executive, political leader, educator, or citizen may dismiss a recommendation by saying: "This isn't a useful recommendation. I am doing that already." But every recommendation I include in the next four chapters was chosen precisely because someone, somewhere, can say: "I am doing that already." Yet that doesn't negate the recommendation. It means instead that more people in more places have to be doing what you are doing, and I would encourage you to help those people, by your example, to adopt the behavior in question.

On to chapter 6, an agenda for business executives . . .

Chapter 6

An Agenda for Business Executives

When my wife, Marie-Louise, introduced me to Joe's Stone Crab of Miami Beach, a favorite of hers from when she had previously lived in South Florida, I was promised a great meal, but I had no idea what an intriguing business experience it was going to be.

Joe's is a rarity: an American restaurant that has prospered for over a century. It is currently the top-grossing independent restaurant in America—despite being the only restaurant in the top 100 that closes for three (and it used to be five) months per year when its principal fare, stone crab, is out of season. Its annual gross is 4 percent greater than that of the second-place competitor, but its monthly gross is 39 percent greater. In a trendy business sector in which the median age of the next ten restaurants on the top 100 list is 27 years, its 116-year run of success is nothing short of astounding.[1] The leading gross certainly suggests efficiency, while the longevity confirms resilience—a productive balance.

I was entranced from the moment I entered the restaurant. The wait staff all stopped to greet us warmly and genuinely. Because I am a business nerd and know that the average annual turnover in the US restaurant industry is 75 percent—which means the average staffer stays for sixteen months—I knew that these folks weren't average.[2] They were invested in the place. We were promptly seated in the main part of the dining room, a space of comfortable elegance with an open second story of generous windows. At the next table was a group of elderly ladies dressed in Sunday best. But behind them was a twentysomething couple, with the woman in a tank top and the man in a short-sleeved shirt. Two more tables over from them, three police officers in uniform chowed down with enthusiasm.

Our waitress, Joan, and the wine steward, Avi, were terrific. I couldn't stop myself from asking: OK, what is going on here? They loved their jobs and the restaurant. Joan told us proudly about her crab pin, which was symbolic of the Waiters Fund. Staff sold the gold pins to raise a reserve for wait staff that come into hard times and need a bit of support. Avi talked about how terrific it was to work at Joe's. Based on our obvious interest in Joe's model, Avi suggested that we talk to fourth-generation co-owner Stephen Sawitz, and helped make that happen.

So, several months later, my wife and I had the pleasure of meeting with Stephen, a tall and affable sixty-one-year-old, and his redoubtable mother, Jo Ann Bass. We started with a tour of the restaurant, including the back of the house, and Stephen greeted every employee warmly by name and made sure to attend to little pieces of business along the way. Jo Ann, a feisty but charming grandmother who came of age in an era when women in business were often relegated to the back seat, had clearly become practiced in making certain her voice was not ignored.[3]

Perhaps because he was born into the business, Stephen was incapable of dividing it into siloes. Employees, purveyors, customers, and community were all present in his and his mother's minds as they spoke about their business. It was a systemic approach. For employees, Joe's had to make it a productive and rewarding life. Take J. T., the maître d', who had been at Joe's since 1971— forty-eight years and counting—and who was one of the three members of the wait staff that Stephen invited to join our conversation. J. T. had come from "a swamp in Louisiana" and had had an acquaintance provide an introduction to Joe's that netted him a job as a pot washer. After a couple years of cheerfully and efficiently washing pots, he became a busboy, and after nineteen more years, he applied to become one of the dining-room captains, and got the job. Holding back tears, he credited Jo Ann for having bet on him and supported his promotion nearly three decades earlier. After another twelve years, he became the maître d' for America's highest-grossing restaurant, and he is still in that position fifteen productive years later.

J. T.'s story is neither new nor unique for Joe's. Joe Weiss, the founder, used to drive his workers home after work, because in his era, African-Americans weren't allowed on Miami Beach after sunset and Joe didn't want it to be impossible for African-Americans to work at his restaurant. In the 1970s, Joe's offered health insurance, pensions, and profit sharing for workers, long before those were common benefits in industry in general, let alone in the laggard restaurant industry. Everybody received an end-of-year bonus. In an industry with 75 percent annual turnover, Joe's hourly employees stay an average of ten years and its overall staff an average of fifteen years. No wonder we had such a wonderful customer experience.

But the system can't work for employees only. It has to work for suppliers too—"purveyors," as Stephen refers to them, using the industry's term. Joe's business is founded on stone crabs, a delicacy that Stephen's great-grandfather and great-grandmother introduced to the dining public. Joe's is by far the biggest purchaser of stone crabs in the country. It operates stone-crab fisheries itself and in addition purchases large quantities of stone crabs from independent fisheries. When we talked about the purveyors, the response was truly systemic. It wasn't just about the current fishermen and -women. "We want our fishermen to be the best paid," Joe said, "so their sons and daughters will want to become our fishermen." This is not narrow reductionism: it is expansiveness. It balances a traditional separation, in which most companies are transactional in their supplier relationships, with a connectedness that acknowledges the interdependence between Joe's system and that of the fishermen supplying Joe's.

Then there are the customers. They can't all afford stone-crab claws, which are an expensive entrée. A medium portion is on the menu at $44.95, a large at $69.95. Claw entrées are the base of the business—for the most part, an innovation of Joe Wiess's. Before him, nobody thought a stone-crab-claw entrée would be worth anything, let alone $45 to $70 a plate. But because of that high price, Joe's insists on having an entrée for customers who want an affordable meal. And that is the fried half-chicken at $6.95—the second-most-purchased entrée after stone-crab claws.

The fried half-chicken is Jo Ann's baby, and she staunchly and proudly refuses to raise the price despite the financial folks insisting to her that it loses the restaurant money with every order and imploring her to approve a price hike. "They say you don't make any money, but you are," she retorts. She knows that if Joe's were to become an elite place featuring only $45–$70 entrées, it would be a different place, and not in a good way. The kids in the tank tops and the cops wouldn't come—and it would be a lesser place for their absence. So, the $6.95 fried half-chicken is a crucial piece of Joe's complex adaptive system.

The same thinking is evident in Stephen's decision twenty-five years ago to change the restaurant layout by putting a large service bar where the original entrance used to be. The reaction internally was that the new bar was so big that it eliminated a number of dining tables, which would reduce revenues. Stephen's reaction: "Exactly, and that is fine." This is an important marker of non-reductionist thinking. Yes, the big bar might reduce the number of tables. But patrons at the main bar wouldn't have bartenders juggling their orders with the drink orders for the tables (the primary function of the service bar). And it would help those waiters get drinks to their table patrons faster and with greater ease. Introducing a friction in the form of a table-cannibalizing bar may have made the restaurant appear less efficient at first blush, but in Stephen's view the move was a no-brainer in the longer term, improving the guest experience and reducing the pressure on both his bartending and wait staff.

Stephen's decision to change the long-standing entrance and add a service bar is part of a pattern at Joe's: experimentation. As of a quarter-century ago or more, it was already obvious that Joe's was a monumental success. A natural reaction would have been to stick with what made Joe's successful. Instead, Stephen has kept on experimenting—whether with a new entrance and outsize service bar, an outdoor dining area, a takeout business, or a summer menu to shrink the summer closure from five months to three. These are thoughtful and reflective, though not traditional, tweaks to a complex adaptive system. Tweaks of this sort ensure that Joe's does not fall prey to believing that it has achieved perfection but instead maintains a continued drive for improvement.

Perhaps most endearingly, the Joe's Stone Crab business model is environmentally sustainable. Stone crabs are not killed in the process of harvesting and selling their claws. Depending on size and sex of the crab, the fisherman can remove one or both of its claws. If the removal is done properly, the stone crab can be returned to the sea where it can survive and regrow its claw or claws. Joe's can take credit for popularizing the only meat meal that doesn't involve killing the animal involved.

Joe's Stone Crab demonstrates that narrow reductionism and the rigid pursuit of proxies for efficiency are not requirements for business success. Considered strictly, Joe's pursues inefficiently high compensation for both employees and suppliers, inefficient use of space in the restaurant, and inefficient sale of low-price chicken entrees. All that notwithstanding, Joe's model has been proven monumentally effective for over a century, with no sign of slowing down. Despite all its apparent inefficiency, Joe's has been financially successful at the highest level while benefiting its workers, suppliers, and community. Its model is consistent with operating a complex adaptive system, not a machine, and it achieves the balances that the system requires.

Joe's outsize success—while that of only one, relatively small business—points to steps that every business executive in every business can take to contribute positively to the future of democratic capitalism rather than serve as a consistently mixed blessing. Business executives need to turn their backs on the dominant vector of reductionism, recognize that slack is not the enemy, guard against surrogation by using multiple measures, and appreciate that monopolization is not a sustainable goal. It will take some time for successes like that of Joe's Stone Crab to cause executives to question their existing, ineffective models. But over time, integrative executives like Stephen will become the rule, not the exception. Once again, each of these agenda items is illustrated with a real example of it happening today, otherwise it wouldn't be on the list.

Turn Your Back on Reductionism

Executives are taught to manage machines. Most have an educational background in business administration or engineering/computer science, or both: nine of the *Fortune* 10 CEOs have either a business or engineering undergraduate degree, and four earned an MBA in addition.[4] This training teaches them to break down their companies into their constituent parts—individual disciplinary pieces—and optimize each piece; all with the assumption that the pieces can be added back up to produce a productive and useful whole. Even if they weren't formally educated that way, they are indoctrinated into that approach the instant they start their careers in business, when they are assigned to a narrow job in an organization that is structured accordingly.

This reductionism has handy elements, to be sure. It makes the resulting narrowly defined jobs much easier to fill, since training employees for them is much simpler. But it also makes employees much less valuable, interchangeable cogs in a big and not very effective machine. This has the effect of generating Pareto compensation outcomes. On the one hand, there is downward pressure on the compensation for the interchangeable cogs, because the candidates with narrow, specialized skills are relatively plentiful and their ability to add true value is constrained by the way they are used ineffectively to produce parts within what is actually a complex adaptive system. Meanwhile, there is an insatiable desire in companies for the rare few magic value creators who know how to perform integrations that are necessary for and consistent with a complex adaptive system. These are the star CEOs, whose compensation price tags know no bounds. This means the majority of employees are driven toward subsistence compensation, and a very few are given whatever it takes to acquire their services.

The results of this managerial reductionism are negative for all stakeholders, producing an unstable, unbalanced Pareto distribution of employee incomes; an unsatisfactory, repetitive existence for most employees; and mediocre outcomes for customers who never want to hear a service professional say, "I can't help you. It is not my job. You need to speak with the [fill in the blank] department." But although none of us likes these outcomes, they all somehow make sense to managers schooled in reductionism.

My challenge to executives, therefore, is to reject this reductionism. As the case of Joe's Stone Crab amply illustrates, the pieces of the business puzzle are all interrelated. The business cannot be reduced, like a machine, to a sum of parts. Managers should instead embrace the reality that a business is a complex adaptive system, in which the components and subsystems are highly interdependent, human processes in which overoptimizing one part compromises optimization of another part and can lead to alienation and disengagement from the people you need to be most engaged.

Four Seasons Hotels and Resorts, the world's most successful luxury hotel chain, is a business that, like Joe's, recognizes these key attributes. Like the restaurant business, the hotel business is characterized by low pay and high employee turnover (over 70 percent annually). That is because those responsible for labor costs and those responsible for the customer experience are in entirely different silos and have narrow goals—and relentless pursuit of the labor cost objective inevitably creates high turnover, which equally inevitably compromises the ability of the hotel staff to deliver a high-quality customer experience.

At Four Seasons, founder Isadore Sharp recognized the tight connection between employees and guest experience and came to believe that the only way the guests were going to receive the kind of luxury service for which he aimed to deliver was if Four Seasons treated its employees like it wanted its employees to treat its guests. As he says, it is his business version of "The Golden Rule." To him, the two things, employee treatment and guest services, are inextricably tied. He recognized that the drive for efficiency in managing staff had separated the people serving from the people served and that he needed to redress the balance by reconnecting them. That's why Four Seasons employees enjoy the best pay, the best eating and changing facilities, the best training, and the best career development in the industry. In addition, even though Four Seasons seeks to win in its segment of the business on the basis of truly exemplary and memorable guest service, it has neither a head of guest experience nor department for guest services. This is because the Four Seasons philosophy is that guest service is everybody's job—again, a system view rather than a mechanistic one.

The result has been the lowest employee turnover, highest employee satisfaction, highest guest satisfaction, and highest profitability among luxury hotel chains worldwide. While reductionist executives at its competitors probably can't imagine how the highest pay could possibly coexist with the highest profitability, Sharp sees this coexistence as the natural consequence of managing his hotels as complex adaptive systems in which everything is connected to everything else.

Recognize That Slack Is Not the Enemy

In the dominant machine-based model, slack, which is equated with waste, must be eliminated in order to maximize the machine's efficiency. As I noted earlier, the management tools we use to do this are based on the techniques originally pioneered by W. Edwards Deming—who would probably turn over in his grave if he knew where we had taken his ideas. There is no doubt that Deming's tools have been a great boon to business efficiency, and their application can contribute to a competitive cost structure, which is necessary for competitiveness. But they can wreak havoc when the drive to eliminate slack is taken too far. Deming himself recognized the systemic complexity of businesses and taught that there is always an optimal level of slack for any business system— and that level is not zero. Slack is a manifestation of friction, of the sort that in the right amounts contributes to greater resilience.

Brazilian private-equity firm 3G Capital is learning this the hard way with its Kraft Heinz investment. Flush with its apparent success in consolidating the global brewing industry with Anheuser-Busch InBev (ABI), 3G successively gained control of Heinz in 2013 and Kraft in 2015 and then engineered a merger of the two food companies. It saw the resulting food conglomerate as bloated and riddled with slack that could be taken out with 3G's zero-based budgeting (ZBB) approach. Under ZBB, each budget year starts with zero costs and every cost item has to be justified one by one. It sounds good in theory and has delivered early cost wins for some 3G Capital companies, including ABI. Initially, Kraft Heinz looked as if it might follow suit. Between 2015 and 2018, ZBB was able to drive sales, general, and administrative (SG&A) costs at the merged company from 10 percent of sales to 8 percent of sales—an impressive 20 percent improvement in overhead-cost efficiency, consistent with an all-out attack on the enemy: slack.[5]

However, it appears in hindsight that some of those costs weren't entirely wasteful slack. During that same period (2015–2018), the gross margin at Kraft Heinz—i.e., revenues less the cost of goods sold as a percentage of sales—fell by 3.5 percentage points, from 39.5 percent of sales to 36 percent of sales. The 2-percentage-point reduction in SG&A costs helped lead to a 3.5-percentage-point reduction in profit margin—a net detriment to the business of 1.5 percentage points. This substantial decay in its business pros-pects forced Kraft Heinz to announce a massive $15.4 billion write-down in its assets in February 2019, one of the ten larg-est corporate write-downs in the decade. 3G Capital is learning an important lesson: serving the customer distinctively at a profit is a goal that requires thoughtful and intelligent slack—friction against efficiency.

So, what does positive friction look like in such situations?

In a body of work that she lays out in her 2014 book, *The Good Jobs Strategy*, MIT/Sloan professor Zeynep Ton studied retailers to understand the implications of staffing decisions for retailer prof-itability and success.[6] In retailing, after the unavoidable cost of the goods on the shelves, the biggest cost is that of the staff who work in the stores. She observed that most retailers had evolved to a model in which minimizing the cost of store staff was a central goal. One way was to pay as low a wage as possible, which is why retail clerk and cashier are among the lowest-wage jobs in America. Still another way is to drive out all slack by reducing the number of store-staff hours to the bare minimum required to serve customers. Increased efficiency through low wages and the elimination of slack is most retailers' theorized success formula.

But a smaller number of retailers—including Costco, Trader Joe's, and QuikTrip—have followed a very different model. In addition to paying much higher wages than customary in the industry and training to a much greater extent than customary, they consciously and deliberately build meaningful slack into their staffing. These are salesperson, clerk, and cashier hours that would be excessive according to the staffing formulas used by their competitors. But rather than being less profitable due to these purposely higher costs, these retailers earn much higher sales per square foot of space and much higher profitability than retailers who follow the standard model. Why? Because customers love the superior service that they receive from cheery and effective workers in a delivery system that features the presence of multiple manifestations of friction. So, when customers need a little bit of extra attention, they get it, from a happy, knowledgeable staff person. These retailers understand that they exist in and are a part of a complex adaptive system. In that system, slack is not an unalloyed enemy and all things that seem like "efficiency" are not necessarily efficient.

Ton's work clearly demonstrates that a model embracing optimal rather than minimal slack does in fact work in retail. She shows that a combination of higher pay, more training (particularly cross-training), greater slack, and limited assortment is the combination that produces extraordinary results in retailing—and has been applied beyond in nursing homes and call centers.

It is clearly doable, and her Good Jobs Institute is helping other retailers to adopt this successful approach—which sees slack as a variable in a complex adaptive system to be balanced rather than as an error to be eliminated.

Manufacturing experts recognize the importance of slack when dealing with the most complex machines, for example the giant industrial paper machines used in making high-volume grades such as photocopier paper or toilet tissue. These machines are actually complex systems that cost hundreds of millions of dollars and have numerous connected steps involving mixing, pressure, heat, and cooling that convert slushy wood pulp into finished paper—at mind-boggling speeds. Operators have come to realize that it is not possible in advance to figure out what will eventually breakdown, but eventually something will. When it does, the breakdown is typically catastrophic, forcing long shutdowns and high costs for repair. Hence, they have found that it is smarter to shut the machine down episodically for preventative maintenance, which introduces slack in the form of downtime, but reduces the likelihood of catastrophic failure.

Managers also need to appreciate that the current budget of any company represents the good and bad of the company's history. It represents the result of the most recent tweak. Scrapping it and starting from scratch is not the answer. Tweaking it again and again and again is the superior approach for a complex adaptive system. It is how the balance between continuity and change gets maintained. In contrast, 3G Capital's ZBB approach, which is beloved by consultants, implicitly assumes that the company is a perfectible machine and that there is nothing really important to be learned from the past. It also defines a perfect state (no slack) and treats this as an achievable goal. As we've seen in the real world, perfection is not achievable and looking for ways to achieve it through some inevitably imperfect model and its related measures is a fool's errand. And that is why the 2-point cost reductions at Kraft delivered a 3.5-point fall in margin.

Guard against Surrogation with Multiple Measurements

As discussed earlier, the surrogation of proxies for models is a natural and dangerous occurrence in general and in the business domain specifically, where it facilitates gaming and makes executives unreflective about how their business really works.

The best defense against a proxy becoming the implicit surrogate for a model is to use multiple measurements as proxies for judging the progress of the model against the goal, in particular proxies that are internally contradictory. Contradictory proxies encourage managers to think integratively and to take a systems perspective on the company's operations. For example, at Wells Fargo, imagine if rather than the single proxy of number of accounts per customer, the proxies had been: number of accounts per customer, activity level per account, growth in customer-bank interactions, and customer retention. More accounts makes it harder to have more activity per account, so number of accounts wouldn't be slavishly pursued. Rather, a balance would need to be targeted. That would mean working harder to make more customers happy rather than trying to acquire more customers who would be unhappy with a lack of attention.

In fact, some companies already do think and operate in that fashion. Since its inception, in 1970, Southwest Airlines has been the most successful airline in America by nearly every accepted measure. It has grown from a tiny local Texas carrier to flying the greatest number of passenger seat-miles in the country. It has been by far the most profitable airline in America for almost half a century. It has a unique low-cost strategy that is heralded by many commentators, including strategy guru Michael Porter, as being a key source of its success—and I agree.

But another thing that contributes to Southwest's striking success is its multiplicity of internally contradictory proxies for success. Southwest seeks to be both the lowest-cost airline in America and the number-one airline in America in customer satisfaction, employee satisfaction, and profitability.[7] That means, for example, that it can't possibly pursue low cost by driving down wage levels and fighting to keep the unions out. (Most people think that Southwest is nonunion, but its unionization rates are similar to those of its competitors.) It has to find cleverer ways to keep control of employee costs. It does so by paying them better per hour than any of its competitors do, while helping employees be so productive that labor costs per passenger seat-mile and as a percentage of revenues are lower, not higher than those at competitors. At first blush it may seem crazy for Southwest to have such internally contradictory proxies for measuring the success of its model. But those contradictory proxies have helped Southwest avoid the surrogation trap.

Had Wells Fargo utilized multiple and internally contradictory proxies like Southwest has, it is unlikely that the company would have gotten into such trouble. The very fact of having four proxies at Southwest (cost, customer satisfaction, employee satisfaction, and profitability) gives a clear indication that no single one of them is equal to the model. It reinforces that these four proxies add up to an approximate measurement of the model's outcomes, not a representation of the model itself. More generally, it recognizes that a system is a complex combination of parts—that move both separately and together—and that success requires maintaining a balance between that connectedness or interdependence of the parts and separation between them.

This approach, while being driven from a different logic, is consistent with the popular concept and tool from Robert Kaplan and David Norton, who (very appropriately from my perspective) called it the "balanced scorecard" in their famous 1992 *Harvard Business Review* article. They argue for multiple, independent proxies for performance, including financial, customer, operational, and innovation proxies.[8] With its (at least somewhat) internally contradictory measures, the "balanced scorecard" approach holds the promise of preventing damaging surrogation of the sort seen at Wells Fargo and in the capital markets generally.

Realize That Monopolization Is Not a Sustainable Goal

Executives dream of becoming the next John D. Rockefeller, who built a monopoly in the oil-refining business in the late nineteenth century. Eliminating the competition feels like a natural goal; it means you've won. That's why Intel attempted to eliminate Advanced Micro Devices, for which it was fined by the European Union.[9] That is why Facebook is using its deep pockets and huge user base to empower its Instagram subsidiary to "kneecap" its rival Snapchat by copying Snapchat's core product.[10] Managers feel more secure when their customers have no alternative to the product or service they produce. Given that American monopolists from Rockefeller to Bill Gates to Mark Zuckerberg have become among the richest men in history, the appeal of establishing a monopoly is understandable. But it has a downside. Monopolies don't last in the natural world, and they don't last in business either.

Monopolies don't last in nature because they don't adapt, and the fundamental rule of nature, as posited by Charles Darwin, is survival of the fittest—by which he meant those most able to adapt to the environment and its changes. And what drives adaptation in business? It is learning from one's customers how to provide better value for them. Customers, not those who serve them, define value. Providers can only hypothesize about what constitutes customer value. Providers learn based on customer feedback, and therefore customer feedback is the linchpin of positive adaptation. It is very difficult to become a better provider of a given product or service in the absence of real customer feedback.

It is not the mere existence of customer feedback that produces positive adaptation. Listening to customer feedback and taking action on it are both necessary preconditions for positive adaptation. But change is never easy. It is tiring and expensive. As a consequence, most companies, most of the time, will listen to customers only when they must, and they have to only when the customer can credibly threaten to become an ex-customer if the provider doesn't listen and change.

Therein lies the fundamental sustainability problem for monopolists. They don't have to listen to their customers. Anybody who has to wait days to get their cable-television service problem fixed recognizes the phenomenon. The monopoly provider of cable TV in your region doesn't have to be responsive, because if you want cable TV, you have no choice but to use that company. In the end, monopolists exist to serve themselves, not to serve their customers. They don't get the training that customers normally provide, because the monopolist doesn't have to train.

As a consequence, monopolies stultify over time. They may have virtually unlimited resources, but they don't have the motivation to deploy them productively. When the environment in which they operate necessitates major adaptation, they are unable to adjust, because they are out of practice. AT&T enjoyed a monopoly on long-distance phone calls in America from the inception of long-distance telephony in the early twentieth century until 1982, when the Justice Department ended AT&T's monopoly on US long-distance telephony. This was a huge and incredibly lucrative market that had made AT&T one of the richest companies in America. As of the allowance of competition, mighty AT&T should have had every advantage imaginable over small, newly empowered competitors like MCI and Sprint. But it struggled to compete, let alone continue to dominate, and experienced a decades-long decline in market share and profitability. Two decades later, in 2005, AT&T was bought by SBC Corporation for $16 billion, a fraction of AT&T's worth in 1993, when it was still the most valuable company in America.[11]

Similarly, Microsoft has had an extremely profitable near-monopoly on personal-computer operating systems since its inception, in 1975. Despite that domination and the resources that came with it, when the prevailing form of personal digital device switched from the personal computer to the smartphone, Microsoft was utterly unable to adapt and has a minuscule 0.3 percent market share of smartphone operating systems—a market dominated by Google Android and Apple iOS. That said, Microsoft deserves full credit for accomplishing something few monopolies have, which is to figure out how to compete very successfully in a different market than its original monopoly market—in Microsoft's case, cloud computing, which will potentially more than make up for the company's failure in mobile operating systems.

If anything, Microsoft's cloud-computing success will be the exception that proves the monopoly rule. Monopolies may be efficient. It is more efficient to have one monopoly set of phone lines crisscrossing America or one set of monopoly coaxial cable wires running from the street to each house in the neighborhood. But monopolists can't adapt, because they are not practiced in responding to the changing tastes and desires of customers. The biggest threat to aforementioned monopoly cable providers is the rising tide of cable cutting—that is, customers deciding that they just don't need cable television at all in a video-streaming world.

Hence, while there is extremely high short-term value in successfully seeking a monopoly position on a given field of play, it plants the seeds of inevitable obsolescence.

The damage occurs in two ways. Resilience is compromised, because with monopolies the drive for improvement simply disappears over time. At the same time, monopolies famously become bloated, because the absence of competition encourages an overaccumulation of slack that benefits the short-term interests of managers, workers, and, often, governments—but certainly not customers—to the extent that the once efficient organization that triumphed over its competitors becomes highly inefficient over time.

A great company needs great competitors to stay great. Of the ten companies that have been a component of the Dow Jones Industrial Average for more than thirty years, nine of the ten (ExxonMobil, Procter & Gamble, United Technologies, 3M, Merck, American Express, McDonald's, Coca-Cola, and Boeing) have always had at least one formidable competitor.[12] The only exception is IBM, which arguably didn't have strong enough competitors for too long a time and is now in a long-term swoon from which it may never recover. Companies should compete aggressively against their competitors; just not with the intent of driving them out of business. That is because the only way to stay sustainably strong is to compete aggressively to win the hearts, minds, and pocketbooks of customers against formidable competition.

That is the case for Joe's Stone Crab. The Lower 48 states comprise 3.1 million square miles of territory, causing one to think, perhaps, that Joe's would be afforded some geographic exclusivity. But that is far from the case. Well within Joe's own square mile is another one of America's highest-grossing restaurants, eleventh-ranked Prime 112. Joe's has no chance to rest on its laurels and stop thinking about serving the customer better, because another one of America's most successful restaurants is only a five-minute walk away.

I learned about the importance of strong competition at a young age from watching and listening to my father. When I was two years old, he started a tiny business called Wallenstein Feed & Supply (WFS) that manufactured and sold animal feed to the farmers in south-central Ontario, Canada. He grew it into a successful business competing against then much bigger competitors, including the local subsidiary of Cargill, a $115 billion behemoth. In due course, he and my older brother, who had by then joined the company, built the biggest single animal-feed mill in Ontario, alongside our smaller original mill, and with that added capacity, WFS vied for Ontario market-share leadership.

Several years later, my brother was pushing my father to build a third mill, still bigger than the second mill, at our production site. My father was very reluctant to build the additional large mill. I asked him if he thought it was too risky. "Not at all," he responded. "I know it would be a big success." Why the reluctance then? It turns out that he didn't want to risk driving his competitors out of business. He told the story of when, during the first decade of the business, his feed mill burned to the ground. His customers needed a source of feed or their animals would have died in relatively short order. It would have been a perfect opportunity for his competitors to swoop in and steal all of his customers. Instead, they produced feed for him to serve his customers. And since feed mills are susceptible to fires (due to the combustible combination of hot-running machinery and fine dust from the feed mixing and production), he did the same for his competitors when the shoe was on the other foot.

My father recognized that a monopoly was not good for the industry. Customers gained value from the redundancy in the system. He wasn't interested in pushing his competitors to the brink.

Our company has built capacity since, but more slowly than it could have, because driving competitors out of business just hasn't been a goal. Today, WFS is the biggest competitor in the industry by a wide margin, but there is healthy competition in the industry that serves farmers well and keeps all of the producers on their toes. Were WFS to let up and get complacent, it wouldn't take long for one of the competitors to displace it—and that helps make sure it doesn't happen.

Creating an environment in which the explicit goal is to eliminate competition is not helpful. Yet it appears to be the goal of a number of today's leading behemoths, including Facebook, Alphabet (parent company of Google), and Amazon. That behavior will promote an unsustainable Pareto structure in the modern economy. Both those companies and their customers would be better off if the companies recognized that monopolies—no matter how efficient at first—are simply not sustainably resilient.

Getting Started

It won't be easy for executives to get started on their agenda. It means unlearning ideas and beliefs that are deeply embedded. The best way to get started is for executives to use themselves as a proxy for the people in whatever system they are attempting to understand and operate.

If they are starting down the path of reductionism by breaking a problem into independent parts, they need to ask themselves: Is that how I think about problems or issues pertaining to myself? To my family? To my friends? Or do I think about problems that affect me in a more holistic manner? And if so, how could I think of this problem holistically as well?

If they are working their way toward the elimination of all slack, they need to ask themselves: How do I feel when I have absolutely no slack and am forced to run from one activity to the next without a break—ever? Do I do my best work under those circumstances, let alone decent work? If not, why should I assume that the process or activity from which I am eliminating all slack will work efficiently?

If they are enthusiastically pursuing the achievement of progress on a given measurement, they need to ask themselves: Do I respond well to being measured on just one single dimension? Or do I prefer and see as more realistic a multifaceted approach? If so, how could I add further attributes to my measurement system to make it something more consistent with how I would want to be measured?

Finally, if they are enthusiastically working toward the elimination of competitors and the achievement of a monopoly position, they need to ask themselves: If there were no consequences to ignoring our customers, would I work hard to listen to the customers and change what we do to make them happy? If not, then what would cause me to believe that if we achieve the sought-after monopoly, we would continue to listen to and respond to customers?

These small things will help executives get started. But executives will need help from political leaders and educators to set a better context in which to leverage their work, and those are the subjects of the next two chapters.

Chapter 7

An Agenda for Political Leaders

September 2008 was a particularly bad month for American political leaders, whether elected politicians or senior government administrators. The financial turbulence that began in 2007 reached a crescendo in September 2008. On September 6, the Treasury Department was obliged to provide a $100 billion bailout for Fannie Mae and Freddie Mac, the federally backed mortgage-guarantee agencies Congress had created in 1938 and 1970, respectively, in order to promote American home ownership. On September 14, Lehman Brothers (of Repo 105 fame) declared bankruptcy due to its heavy exposure to mortgage-backed bonds, having failed to obtain a bailout from the Federal Reserve Bank and the Treasury, which deemed the investment bank small enough to fail. Just two days later, however, the impending collapse of insurance giant American International Group (AIG) forced the Federal Reserve to intervene with an initial $85 billion bailout (later increased). On September 25, the Office of Thrift Supervision seized Washington Mutual, the country's largest savings-and-loan bank and placed it into receivership.

Three days later, on September 28, Congress refused to approve the more comprehensive bailout program, the Troubled Asset Relief Program (TARP). That rejection precipitated a 777.68-point drop in the Dow Jones Industrial Average on September 29, the biggest drop in history to that point, forcing Congress to reverse course, with the eventual passage of TARP on October 3. But the damage to confidence had already been done. Between September 19 and October 10, the Dow dropped 31 percent—the biggest one-month drop since another miserable fall month on Wall Street: September 1929. Banks stopped lending, even to their best clients. Commercial-paper programs, which had become a key source of short-term funding for large companies, stopped being supported by the financial intermediaries, threatening the solvency of even blue-chip industrials.[1] America's six largest banks all received assistance ranging from $10 to $25 billion from the TARP program to ensure their solvency and their continued ability to provide service to their customers.[2] Nonetheless, the economy went into deep recession and unemployment soared, leading to one of the slowest economic recoveries in US history.

The six biggest US banks that received TARP funding are the first, second, third, fourth, seventh, and eighth largest banks in North America. On the same list, Canada's "Big 5" banks ranked fifth, sixth, ninth, tenth, and eleventh.[3] But unlike the six big US banks (and many smaller US banks), the five big Canadian banks did not receive or require bailout money from their government. Despite its close proximity to and interdependence with the US economy, the Canadian financial system did not experience a crisis of confidence and did not require the huge bank bailout programs that took place in the United States and most of the world's advanced economies—from that of the United Kingdom to those of most of Europe and Australia.[4]

There were of course many factors behind this difference; there is never just one. But at the very least Canada's policy approach to this vital sector has to be considered as one important factor, for it is very different from the US approach—in ways that implicitly recognize the financial system as a complex adaptive system and in ways that inform the agenda I propose here for political leaders. The first point of difference is that regulation is not seen as providing solutions so much as improving financial practice.

From Solutions to Improvements

The most important and comprehensive financial regulatory legislation in Canada is the Bank Act, which was enacted in 1871, four years into Canada's life as a sovereign country. The Bank Act came with a very unusual provision: a required decennial review. Regardless of the situation, regardless of the political context, the act was to be formally reviewed every ten years. While historians are not clear on how the Bank Act came to contain the decennial-review provision, they believe it was requested by the banks themselves, with speculation that bank leaders at the time felt that the periodic review would keep them better connected to their customers.

In any case, ever since 1871, the Bank Act has been periodically reviewed and tweaked to maximize its future effectiveness. In fact, in 1992 the review interval was shortened to five years. As a consequence, there will never be a big partisan political fight over whether or not to "repeal and replace" the Bank Act. It is thoroughly reviewed just because five years have passed. This has enabled Canada's regulators to balance continuity with change, tweaking regularly so that the system never becomes unbalanced.

In addition, the regulatory oversight in Canada is much more relationship-based than rule-based. Canada's top regulator during the global financial crisis and its aftermath was Julie Dickson, Superintendent of OSFI (the Office of the Superintendent of

Financial Institutions). She was well known for her habit of flying regularly from her Ottawa office to Toronto to meet with the CEOs of the five big Canadian banks. No one but Dickson and the CEOs knows exactly what went on during those one-on-one discussions. But the rumor on Bay Street (Canada's equivalent of Wall Street) was that Dickson was not shy in offering her opinions, most notably in suggesting that the banks would be unwise to emulate their US counterparts in fueling a housing bubble by offering easy long-term fixed-rate mortgages. In a 2010 article, Dickson herself stressed the importance of informal oversight of this kind: "Rules—such as minimum capital requirements, leverage ratios, limits on activities—are important, but in the Canadian experience, the actual day-to-day supervisory oversight of financial institutions is just as significant . . . Stricter rules, like substantially higher capital requirements, can create a false sense of security; an institution will never have enough capital if there are material flaws in its risk management practices. That is why supervision matters."[5]

From the Parts to the Whole

In the United States, the various financial institutions are regulated by a veritable crazy quilt of narrowly-focused federal and state bodies, all operating independently of each other and jealously guarding their separate patches. Nobody has the mandate to take a holistic, systems approach to the oversight of US financial institutions. If the system fails, everybody can and will attempt to argue that it wasn't because they failed to manage their little part of the system.

Canada is very different. Since 1987, there has been just a single regulator of financial institutions: OSFI. To be sure, within OSFI there are specialized departments focusing on the different parts of the system, but the fact that they are all part of the same agency makes coordination and information sharing much easier and largely eliminates the federal/state/sector distinctions characterizing the US regulatory system. As a result, OSFI can take a broader system view on financial institutions than any US regulator can. In effect, the Canadian regulatory system mirrors the connectedness of the different parts of the real financial system—not the partitioned, reductive construct assumed in US legislation—and that makes it easier for Canadian regulators to see when a dysfunction in one part may have systemwide effects.

From Global Pressure to Local Friction

Finally, the big Canadian banks were not allowed to merge. Two pairs of the five—Royal Bank of Canada and Bank of Montreal, TD Bank and Canadian Imperial Bank of Commerce—attempted to do so in 1998. They argued that in order to compete in an ever more intensely competitive global market, they needed the increased efficiency that would come from merging, taking out redundant costs, and increasing their competitive heft. The Finance Minister at the time, Paul Martin, thought otherwise and refused to allow the two mergers—which would have resulted in two banks controlling approximately 70 percent of Canada's banking assets.[6] And despite the bank leaders' dire warnings at the time about how hard it would be to keep up with global competitors due to the disallowance of the mergers, the Canadian banks in question rank higher on the lead tables now than in 1998, in part because in the lead-up to and through the global financial crisis, they were focused on banking while the big US banks were focused on merging.

Public policy in Canada with regard to banking provides a number of pieces of the agenda for balancing efficiency and resilience in a complex adaptive system. It features continuous tweaking instead of fixed, permanent rules. It takes a holistic perspective rather than many reductionist ones. And it is willing to enforce productive friction to offset the constant pressure for ever more efficiency. Let's look in more detail at these and other shifts in the Canadian approach to policy making and regulating that US political leaders should consider as they contemplate how they can restore balance to democratic capitalism.

Write Revision into the Laws You Make

When Americans identify a problem, their typical reaction is that there should be a law or a rule about it. The United States passes lots of laws and issues many rules as a result. Sadly, the economy doesn't appear to present problems that are permanently fixable. As I pointed out in chapter 4, US policy makers imagined that the Sarbanes–Oxley Act, or SOX, would prevent large-scale corporate abuse. We saw how that worked out, so why should we have assumed that the Dodd–Frank Act of 2010 would succeed in fixing the system where SOX had failed? It, too, was designed to be the comprehensive fix. Yet it has already been dramatically altered, with much controversy around the alterations, in part because it was designed to be permanent.

Once again, the explanation and the solution lie in realizing that the economy and the business world are complex adaptive systems, which quite simply adapt. In other words, when problems recur in natural systems, they are never quite the same as they were before. We can protect people against all the flu viruses we know, but we can't guard against the next adaptation of the virus. We can similarly protect people against the exact repeat of past corporate abuses. But because the players in the system adapt their behavior to game the new legislation, the next banking crisis is not going to be an exact replica of the last. What's more, establishing complicated rules for a game understood in its entirety by no one will inevitably offer opportunities for gaming from the start—in part because the consent of would-be gamers is necessary for the law to pass in our democratic system. Even if that can be avoided and the rules do work at first, players will sooner or later find ways around them because they will have many more years to benefit from the gaming, since no one will have the time, patience, or energy to reengage with lawmaking on the subject again—absent another crisis. Legislative permanence plays right into the hands of the gamers and creates more investment in gaming than would otherwise be the case.

In the natural model of the economy, regulation should be treated less as a cure and more as an exercise in learning and development. And that was the extraordinary insight of the framers of the first Canadian Bank Act. In building in a requirement for a regular revision, Canadian lawmakers were implicitly treating the new law not as a solution but as a prototype from which learning would take place based on the interaction between the prototype and the complex adaptive system it enters. Take encouragement in the learning that comes from experiencing and observing the flaws in action. Then tweak and tweak to make that prototype better and better until it is genuinely good—maybe even close to perfection. In essence, it means policy makers should act like software companies: promise imperfection followed by speedy fixes. In that industry, if customers prefer to get the software early, they receive it knowing it will come with bugs: that isn't a surprise. If instead customers don't want bugs, they are free to wait for later releases. That system works for all customers and for the software producers.

Every new piece of legislation dealing with the economy should be made subject to periodic review and sunsetting if it doesn't pass muster in such a review. This will raise the cost and lower the value of gaming by shortening the period during which the profits from gaming can be accumulated.

On occasion, America does engage in tweaking or sunsetting legislation. The aforementioned TARP is a good example. Under TARP, the Fed was authorized to spend up to $700 billion to purchase troubled assets that were originally defined as residential or commercial loans in default, loans that were threatening the solvency of the financial institutions that held them. The definition was later expanded to include any financial instruments the purchase of which would provide financial-market stability. The program was later cut back to $435 billion and ended up disbursing a little over $400 billion.[7] To the surprise of almost everyone involved, TARP ultimately didn't cost the taxpayers a penny, because the Treasury turned a $15 billion profit on the program—even though the assumption going into the program was that all $700 billion would be spent without any recoveries.[8] And, once the crisis had passed, TARP came to an end.

Other domains provide even better examples, notably in sport. While the National Football League (NFL) is of course no paragon of virtue with its misbehaving players and physical brutality, it does understand and internalize the detrimental gaming of its very valuable game—even totally legitimate gaming by clever coaches. Its standing Competition Committee meets after every season to take stock of how the rules in place did or didn't provide an optimal outcome on the field for the fans. It has the mandate to tweak—and in fact routinely does tweak—the rules that govern play on the field every year. The committee tweaks the rules to keep offense and defense in relative balance, because if the two get out of balance, the game will become more predictable and less exciting for the fans. If offenses starts to dominate defenses, the game will become a back-and-forth offensive race down the field, while if defenses dominate offenses, games will end with no or low score. Both are less enjoyable outcomes than a rough balance between offense and defense. Thanks in part to this relentless tweaking of the game, the NFL has become the most popular and lucrative sports league in America.

Nothing lasts forever—but much legislation implicitly assumes that it does. The assumption should be that all games get gamed and need to be designed for continuous tweaking. The Canadian Bank Act, TARP, and the NFL Competition Committee show that it can be done successfully, and any government actor can follow suit.

Seek Mental Proximity When Designing Policy

Systems-theorist professor John Sterman reminds us that everything we think, do, or say is on the basis of a model. Hence policy makers have no choice but to model their citizens when they design policy for them. However, there is a choice of how they can do that. That model of people can be informed by mental distance from or proximity to those citizens.

In the former camp, we can make general assumptions about "what poor people need" or "what single mothers need" or "what will influence Wall Street executives," and then build complex and highly theoretical models on those assumptions to determine how to legislate and regulate. Unfortunately, although this approach has a pleasing formal rigor about it (it is, after all, how we construct mathematical models), what comes out of it is often highly flawed.

I recall vividly a small example from my time serving on the board of a world-leading nonprofit pediatric hospital in Ontario. The Ministry of Health, which oversees all public hospitals in Ontario, had mandated that hospital CEO compensation packages contain some incentive compensation based on measurable patient objectives, and the board was considering a package for our CEO that contained measurable objectives for the rate of infant patient mortality at the hospital. If she achieved a sufficiently low infant-mortality rate, she would earn a significant additional bonus. By the conclusion of the board discussion, I had little confidence that the compensation committee had determined that our CEO would actually find this incentive motivational.

The CEO had begun her illustrious career low on the hospital totem pole as a nurse, and through hard work, dedication, and native intelligence, had made her way up to the top. By the time of this compensation decision, she was a very successful and revered leader. When I later asked her whether she would be motivated by the infant-mortality-rate target, I knew what her response would be before she gave it: "I can understand why the board would want to install performance incentives into our compensation system. The Ministry of Health is asking for something on that front. But since I began here as a twenty-three-year-old nurse, I have dedicated my life to minimizing the number of babies who die in our care. Nothing the board says or does, no amount of compensation, will change by one iota the dedication with which I pursue my goal of helping every baby who arrives at our hospital leave as healthy as possible."[9]

To be sure, the ministry policy change made sense and was consistent with prevailing compensation theory. But what resulted didn't take into account the real person sitting in the CEO chair, a real person who would have been happy to answer any question we asked her in advance of designing a compensation package that insulted her more than it motivated her.

Given the likelihood that traditional, theory-based approaches will produce deeply flawed outcomes such as this, policy makers will be well advised to shift to an alternative approach, one that is informed by up-close observation and interaction with real citizens. Such an approach is much more likely to generate adaptable prototypes for legislation and regulation that will fit the needs and features of the target population.

It's relatively easy to go talk to a CEO about a compensation plan, of course. But what about a big government initiative affecting thousands, even millions, of people? That's been successfully done. In 2010, when the UK government was putting together what turned out to be the massively successful GOV.UK website service that went live in 2012, the cabinet office created a unit called government digital services (GDS). The new unit was led by Michael Bracken and Tom Loosemore, whose first task was to convince the various government departments and agencies, which collectively produced hundreds of UK government websites, that the true customer of the websites wasn't the departments and agencies themselves but rather the citizens that the departments and agencies were set up to serve.[10]

Even then, the customers that the website producers cared almost exclusively about were those who could make their lives most miserable: reporters and think tanks, who from time to time would criticize what they either saw or failed to see on a government website. Because they had a voice, they scared the government officials. Bracken and Loosemore set out to find out what citizens who didn't have such a voice wanted and needed from government websites, rather than design their solution based on satisfying the agencies and departments or mollifying reporters and think tanks.

Their first initiative was to do a quantitative study of the search data produced by ordinary citizens' visits to UK government websites. When they published their initial results, they came under withering attack in a blog by a qualitative-research expert named Leisa Reichelt. Rather than defend or double down on their existing model, they did the opposite and hired Reichelt to be GDS's head of user research. Bracken and Loosemore credit Reichelt with integrating deep qualitative user research into all GDS work. Through the first year of design, GDS did in-depth ethnographic interviews of hundreds of citizens, watched them use the existing sites, and had them try out initial designs of new sites. Reichelt insisted that the whole team—from developers to designers to product managers—watch the entire videos of the relevant citizen interviews before coming up with design plans. At first Bracken and Loosemore worried that sitting through entire videos would be excessively time consuming. But they soon came to understand the profound value.

Loosemore tells of a particularly striking insight from an interview of a woman in her forties from the northern United Kingdom on the topic of replacing her passport—one of the many reasonably high-volume citizen use cases. As he explained, there are two very different processes one must follow, depending on whether one loses a passport or has it stolen. The latter, for example, involves filing a police report, which is not part of the process for the former. Because of the major differences, the beta version of this service had two entirely separate landing pages: one for if you typed *stolen passport* into the search box, the other for if you typed *lost passport*.

The woman in question told the interviewer the traumatic story of having recently had her passport stolen, so the interviewer had her test the system unprompted and encouraged her to proceed with a search. Loosemore watched in amazement as she typed in *lost passport* and was taken to the newly designed landing page for lost passports. Only then did he realize that in her mind she indeed had "lost" her passport, in that she had it before it was stolen and didn't have it now. Thus, it was "lost" to her. She had no way of knowing in advance the consequences of typing the word *lost* versus *stolen*, which was that she was guided down a track that would not result in getting a new passport anytime soon. After lots of online form filling, she would realize that she needed to find the process for a stolen passport. As a result of watching this user actually interact with the design, the team reversed course and created a single landing page for a person typing either the term *lost passport* or *stolen passport*. On that page, users would find detailed descriptions that would help clarify which button to click—stolen or lost—to get to the process that matched with their needs.

Interestingly to me, Loosemore used the term *friction* to describe what they did in that instance. They initially had a goal of taking out all the friction and getting visitors directly to "lost" or "stolen." The additional combined landing page was what he called "a speed bump on the way." Going a bit slower ended up saving time! The insight from the passport case was applied to other services. For example, for the service of acquiring power of attorney (typically gotten by a son or daughter on behalf of an aging parent), they put in a speed bump that forced applicants to go back to their family and ask a number of questions before plowing ahead with the application, because the user researchers found that if those conversations didn't happen, there could be deep resentment over who got power of attorney over what. Here again, pursuit of unalloyed efficiency was suboptimal. Balancing the pressure for fewest clicks with friction by way of speed bumps produced a high enough level of efficiency but also resilience in terms of not inadvertently leading people down unproductive paths.

Achieving mental proximity to users helped the GDS team reduce the hundreds of UK government websites to a single site—GOV.UK—with usability that is now considered a global standard. In 2013, the site won the design of the year at the Design Museum awards, the United Kingdom's most prestigious design award for all entities across the entire country, not just government. In fact, in its eleven years thus far, the award has gone to a government agency only once: GOV.UK.

Dial Up Productive Friction in Trade

As we saw earlier, the prevailing wisdom in policy circles has long been that lowering trade barriers is an unalloyed good. That is why, since 1947, the United States has pushed for freer trade, through the General Agreement on Tariffs and Trade as well as through bilateral and (with Canada and Mexico) trilateral agreements. The country, moreover, has led by example, making its own economy perhaps the world's most open marketplace. By and large that leadership has been necessary, because back in 1950, when average trade tariffs stood at 25 percent of the value of goods traded, the balance between efficiency and friction in trade was unquestionably too far in the direction of friction. Productive countries were operating way below capacity, to the detriment of all but a very few of their citizens.

At today's 4 percent, however, it is legitimate to question whether America has overcompensated. To begin with, although free trade does benefit the overall economies of the partners, it most certainly does not benefit everyone in the economies in question. As economist Dani Rodrik points out, there are always losers from trade, and in a developed country like the United States, the loser is overwhelmingly unskilled labor. Although economists have historically judged such losses to be small and not consequential, more recent work demonstrates that they are of meaningful and permanent size. For example, in the decade following the passage of the North American Free Trade Agreement, high-school dropouts in locales whose employers were heavily affected by imports experienced wage growth of 8 percentage points lower than those of their counterparts in locales whose industries were not similarly affected. Overall wage growth in industries that experienced a loss in their protection from imports fell 17 percentage points relative to those in industries not experiencing a loss in protection.[11]

Contributing to this imbalance is the fact that American trade policy is in fact far freer than that of its trading partners. Virtually every major developed country restricts competition in sensitive sectors of its economy in numerous ways. Canada, for example, notionally allows foreign banks to "compete" in its market, but the subtle array of restrictions on foreign banks has enabled the five big Canadian banks to dominate their home market—while growing to substantial size in the attractive, sizable, and quite open US banking market. And while US automakers can in theory export cars into the very large Japanese car market duty free, US car exports to Japan are close to nil. There are myriad nontariff restrictions that dramatically raise the cost of selling an American-made car in Japan, from safety inspections to zoning regulations for dealers. As a result, while Japan exports over 1.7 million automobiles to the United States in a year, the United States exports just 17 thousand to Japan.[12] Some argue that this is because American vehicles are not competitive in Japan. But it is not just American vehicles. Japan has managed to keep foreign-vehicle penetration of its home market under 10 percent—a strikingly low share to be sure, and one out of step with all other advanced markets, including that of car-producing neighbor South Korea.[13] Yes Japan makes great cars: but not that great! The list goes on and on. The European Union protects farmers. France protects yogurt. China protects whatever it feels like protecting with absolutely no apology.

The point is that, going forward, America's political leaders should become more careful about removing trade frictions than they have been. In a complicated world, what seems a barrier to efficiency to one group of players is a necessary protection for the livelihoods of another group of players. For America, it probably is time to take a pause on further opening of its economy to more unfettered trade. It is the world's biggest internal market and already the most open economy of any size in the world. America doesn't need more free-trade deals. It needs to reestablish the faith of its citizens in democratic capitalism with more balance between pressure and friction when it comes to trade policy.

Fight the Giants

Antitrust policy was initiated with the passage of the Sherman Antitrust Act in 1890, which sought to counteract industry-based Pareto outcomes in which one participant gained such a dominant position that it would have the capacity to reap a disproportionate amount of the rewards from that industry. Now, when we need antitrust enforcement more than ever, our antitrust enforcement is weaker than it has been since its inception, largely thanks to the growing perception that today's would-be monopolists will be so efficient that we will all benefit.

What that argument ignores is that the motive behind the original antitrust legislation was not the impact of monopolization on efficiency, whether positive or negative. In fact, the assumption behind public utilities, like power and water, has always been that having a monopoly will surely be more efficient than having a number of smaller competitors replicating one another's investments and cost structures. Rather, the fundamental concern was the accumulation of power by the producer over the customer. So, our policy was to allow public-utility monopolies in domains such as electricity and water, but then strictly regulate those monopolies in order to counterbalance their market power. To remove regulations purely on the basis of efficiency, therefore, is to misunderstand and even negate what antitrust legislation was designed to do in the first place, which is to prevent the most efficient player from abusing its power.

And I'm afraid those players are doing exactly that. The argument that the technology companies that preside over two-sided monopolies aren't hurting consumers because their service is free is misguided. In a two-sided market, there are—as the name indicates—two sets of customers. For Google, for example, on one side is the search-engine user and on the other side is the advertiser seeking to communicate with that searcher. To say that Google couldn't be causing harm as a monopolist because it doesn't charge anything to the first customer is embarrassingly naive.[14] The other set of customers—who increasingly get gouged as Google becomes more of a monopolist (or in fact a duopolist with Facebook) in the online-advertising market—matter as much as the first set in the two-sided market. It is no virtue to give something away to a certain audience so as to be able to gouge another audience.

On top of this, as pointed out previously, monopolies, whether in the private or public sector, tend to serve their customers increasingly badly as time passes, because they cannot learn from their customers. In addition, monopolies produce brittle monocultures that are vulnerable to an external shock—often from the development of a new technology that the monopolist has ignored for too long because of excessive investment in the status quo.

Robust antitrust enforcement can reduce these risks, because it protects innovative firms the monopolist would otherwise acquire. This may result in some inefficiency in the short term, but giving customers a choice forces the efficient incumbent to listen to consumers, thereby protecting its own dynamic efficiency over the long term and making all companies more alive to the opportunities presented by innovation. The sacrifice of efficiency today is, therefore, an investment in a more robust, resilient, and innovative system over the long term. The efficiency defense should be relegated to the dustbin of history, and policy makers should ensure that antitrust laws return to their original purpose of serving as a deterrent to monopoly outcomes, regardless of short-term efficiency gains.

On this front, the European Union can be seen as a positive example. Despite, as a matter of policy, having adopted the efficiency defense around the time America did, it has been much more forceful in tackling monopolistic behavior on the part of the technology giants.

It has taken on Google's monopolistic practices in three matters over the past three years, fining the company €8.2 billion in the process. The most recent fine, in June 2019, was for €1.5 billion for the classically monopolistic practice of forcing customers of its AdSense service to sign contracts agreeing to accept no advertising from Google's search-engine rivals.[15] The practice plainly and simply sought to eliminate competition through the use of market power. It was indeed making Google more efficient to extract the maximum level of earnings from the EU online-advertising market. This fine followed two others in the preceding two years. One, a record fine of €4.3 billion, was for abusing its dominant position in mobile. The other, a fine of €2.4 billion, was for surreptitiously manipulating search results to the benefit of Google itself and to the cost of unsuspecting searchers. That adds up to three fines totaling €8.2 billion, or nearly $10 billion, for engaging in practices that benefited Google and its efficiency but produced more Pareto results that are bad for democratic capitalism, not only in the European Union but also the rest of the world.

The above enforcement is in the services sector. In addition, the European Union recently took on a big technology manufacturer, Qualcomm, the world's number-one chipmaker. In 2018, the European Union fined Qualcomm €997 million for paying Apple to use only Qualcomm chips—an attempt to try to drive Intel and others out of the mobile-phone-chip business. In 2019, the European Union fined Qualcomm another €242 million for knowingly and purposely selling certain of its chips below cost in order to drive British phone-chip maker Icera out of business. In the end, though, Qualcomm succeeded, because struggling Icera was acquired by larger chipmaker Nvidia, which then shut down the targeted chip business.

The European Union demonstrates that if a jurisdiction reaches beyond the short-sighted efficiency defense, it can successfully target modern monopolists, including the technology giants. America could do the same and strike a blow against Pareto outcomes, if it just made the effort.

Extend Time Horizons

As presently constructed and regulated, the capital markets are feeding, encouraging, forcing, and rewarding short-term, antiresilient behavior. I described earlier how the pressure for company executives to meet or beat their quarterly-guidance, analyst-consensus earnings has become unrelenting. In a downright scary study, finance professors John Graham, Campbell Harvey, and Shiva Rajgopal confirm this. They surveyed four hundred financial executives from large US public companies and found that a majority of the executives agreed that in order to meet the current quarter's analyst-consensus earnings, they would defer or cancel attractive projects.[16] These managers live in fear of an "activist investor" showing up in their share register and exerting pressure on the company to improve its financial performance.

And while these investors usually claim to be interested in the long-term performance of their targets, they actually don't care. Their holding periods are short—422 days on average for American activist hedge funds.[17] At the same time, executive tenure is getter shorter. Median CEO tenure in large public companies has continued to drop, from six years to a new low of five years between 2013 and 2017.[18] So, both predator and prey are becoming more oriented to the short term. The result shows up in the pursuit of short-term efficiency proxies like workforce reduction, outsourcing, and off-shoring—proxies that are destroying companies' longer-term competitiveness and resilience to external shocks.

For this reason, policy makers need to encourage capital providers to pursue longer-term rewards from the companies in which they invest and to utilize more—and more intelligent—long-term proxies for measuring the companies' progress. Here we can see that the Securities and Exchange Commission (SEC) has recently set a good example with its approval of the Long-Term Stock Exchange (LTSE) as the nation's fourteenth stock exchange, in May 2019. Founded by Silicon Valley entrepreneur and best-selling author of *The Lean Startup*, Eric Ries, the LTSE will explicitly require companies that list on the exchange and investors that trade on it to follow practices that are oriented toward the longer term.[19] While the exact listing rules had not been made public as of this writing, they hold the promise of an alternative stock market for both companies and investors who would like to think longer term.

The SEC's approval didn't come easily. There was a fierce and protracted resistance from industry players who benefit from the existing market setup. These were the players who had fought the SEC's earlier approval of the Investors Exchange (IEX), in 2016.

The IEX was specifically set up to offer an exchange that did not enable high-frequency trading. The founding group, led by CEO Brad Katsuyama, believed that high-frequency traders (HFTs) enjoyed an unfair advantage over ordinary investors by setting up trading systems—as exemplified by the leased server space in the NYSE's Mahwah facility—that routed their trades to exchanges faster, thereby enabling HFTs to profit before other traders could react.[20] That is, HFTs had gamed the game for their own advantage, to the disadvantage of traders like the mutual-fund companies and pension funds that invest on behalf of average American families. In addition, the impact of the wild trading activity on the stock prices of companies makes it harder for executives to manage companies for the long term.

To put a constraint on this hyperefficient trading process, the IEX installed a "speed bump." All trades to the IEX need to be routed through a thirty-eight-mile coil of fiber-optic cable that slows quotes and trades by 350 millionths of a second, which is long enough to eliminate the advantage of the HFTs.[21] While IEX is still small—approximately 3 percent of US stock-trading volume—it provides a viable alternative to the traditional big exchanges (the NYSE and NASDAQ) in which HFTs have an advantage over traditional investors.

Another tool that US policy makers could borrow from European countries, including France, Italy, and Belgium, is tenure-based voting rights. In France, for example, the 2014 Florange Act gives shareholders two votes for every share of stock in a given company if they hold that stock for more than two years.[22] The theory behind tenure-based voting rights of this kind is that common equity is supposed to be a long-term stake: once it is given, the company notionally has the capital forever. In practice, anybody can buy that equity on a stock market without the company's permission, which means that it can be and often is a short-term investment. But long-term capital is far more helpful than short-term capital to a company trying to create and deploy a long-term strategy. If you give me one thousand dollars to invest in my business but say that you can change with twenty-four hours' notice how I am allowed to use it, that capital isn't nearly as valuable to me as if you say I can use it as I see fit for ten years. If Warren Buffett's desired holding period for stock is, as he jokes, "forever," while the quantitative arbitrage hedge fund Renaissance Technologies holds investments for only milliseconds, Buffett's equity capital is more valuable than that of Renaissance.

The difference in value to the company notwithstanding, the two types of equity investments are given exactly the same rights, which is a mismatch that tenure-based voting rights are designed to remedy. The tenure-based voting-rights measures in Europe are fairly new, and companies are generally able to opt out of the provisions, so the data on the relative success of these measures is not yet clear. However, these examples show that such initiatives can be put into place legislatively.

I would go further than France, because two years is not long-term enough to enable management teams to take consequential action, and doubling of voting rights is not enough to make a meaningful difference. Instead, I would give the owner of each common share one vote per day of ownership up to four thousand days, or just under eleven years. If you held one hundred shares for four thousand days, you could vote four hundred thousand shares. If you sold those shares, the buyer would get one hundred votes on its day of purchase. If the buyer became a long-term holder, eventually that would rise, to a maximum of four hundred thousand votes. But if the buyer were an activist hedge fund like Pershing Square, whose holding period is measured in months, the interests of long-term investors would swamp its influence on strategy, quite appropriately. Allocating voting rights in this way would reward long-term shareholders for providing the most valuable kind of capital. And it would make it extremely hard for activist hedge funds to take effective control of companies, because each time the hedge funds turned over their stock holdings, their voting rights would be minimized.

Some argue that the net effect of such a regime would entrench bad management. It would not. Currently, investors who are unhappy with management can sell their economic ownership of a share along with one voting right. Under the proposed system, unhappy investors could still sell their economic ownership of a share along with one voting right. But if many shareholders are *happy* with management and yet a single activist hedge fund wants to make a quick buck by forcing the company to sell assets, cut investment in research and development, or take other actions that could harm the company's future, that activist would have a reduced ability to collect the voting rights to push that agenda. Instead, management would be empowered to pursue more-resilient long-term proxies for performance.

Return to More-Progressive Tax Rates

This agenda item is different from the others, all of which are aimed at preventing Pareto outcomes in the first instance. This one is aimed at moderating Pareto outcomes that already exist. As such it is inherently less effective, but I believe that it should be part of the overall agenda for policy makers. It is time to accept that the current, four-decade-long experiment with historically low marginal effective tax rates on very high incomes hasn't produced the promised results.

Let me begin with a brief recap of the history of personal income tax in the United States. Federal income tax, with a top rate of 15 percent, came into existence in 1916, but the top rate rose rapidly to 77 percent by 1918 in order to fund US participation in World War I. After the war ended, the top rate fell back to 25 percent during the 1920s. Then, during the Great Depression, in order to fund the New Deal programs designed to stimulate the economy and provide more assistance to the disadvantaged, the top rate soared again, to 63 percent. Arguably, during this period, taxing the incomes of the rich in order to fund programs for the poor came to be seen by the majority of the electorate, though by no means all, as a legitimate function of government.

When the Second World War came along, rather than being in a position to heighten income taxation from a low base (15 percent) as was the case during the First World War, America needed to raise the top income-tax rate from its already elevated Great Depression level to new highs—to a peak of 94 percent in 1944.

As happened after the First World War, the top rate drifted downward thereafter, but remained above 70 percent through the 1970s. Then, during the Reagan presidency, 1981–1989, the progressivity of the personal-income-tax system was dramatically lessened. The top rate plummeted from 70 percent, which had been its level from 1965 to 1980 (with slight short-term bumps upward in 1968, 1969, and 1970), to 28 percent by the end of Reagan's presidency. That was a low range not seen in America since the period spanning 1925–1931.[23]

Thus, for the half-century from 1932 to 1981, the progressivity of the federal personal-income-tax system featured a top rate perpetually in excess of 63 percent and on average 80 percent. This was a period of exceptional US economic growth and progress for the median family in America. Arguably, that half-century experiment with progressive taxes worked well. Yet despite this economic success, the view emerged that the high marginal tax rates for the highest-earning Americans discouraged their work effort and hurt American growth. This led to the Economic Recovery Tax Act of 1981, which—among other measures—cut the top marginal personal-income-tax rate from 70 percent to 50 percent. That was followed by the Tax Reform Act of 1986, which cut the top rate to 28 percent, roughly a level last seen in 1931.

It is easy to see these two acts as the doings of a conservative Republican President—and indeed the tax-cutting movement was spurred by Ronald Reagan, who campaigned on it in both 1980 and 1984. However, when both acts were passed, the Democrats held large majorities in the House of Representatives (242 to 192 in 1981, and 253 to 182 in 1986). The Republicans had a small majority (53 seats) in the Senate at the time of both acts. The 1981 act was passed by a vote of 282 to 95 in the House and 67 to 8 in the Senate, meaning that almost 100 House Democrats voted in its favor.[24] The 1986 act was the deeper cut, taking the rate down from 50 percent to 28 percent. For that bill, the House vote was a huge majority, 292 to 136, and the Senate vote was 74 to 23. Both votes were overwhelmingly supported by the respective Democratic caucuses. Democrats voted 176 to 74 in favor in the House and 33 to 12 in the Senate. In fact, House Democrats were more favorably inclined toward the act (at 70 percent) than were House Republicans (at 65 percent).[25]

The votes illustrate the power of metaphors and models. The metaphor that carried the day was "trickle down." In the model based on this metaphor, wealthy Americans would work harder and invest more, which would create significantly more economic activity, and the benefits of that increased activity would trickle down to the rest of the American income distribution. That is, those in the rest of the income distribution would benefit more from top-income Americans keeping a much larger portion of their income and generating economic activity than they would if those Americans turned it over to the government to provide it to the rest of the income distribution through transfers.

It was a compelling model, compelling enough to cause a majority of the Democratic Congressional Caucus to vote to support it. But in due course, as we have seen, the model was overwhelmed by the reality that having wealth is causally linked to acquiring more wealth still. And as has been pointed out, when effects become the causes of more such effects, the outcome migrates toward Pareto.

In the modern economy, high-end talent is becoming ever more capable of extracting high pretax earnings by utilizing that talent.[26] When that is combined with a personal-income-tax regime that allows that talent to keep a much larger percentage of its pretax income (relative to rates that prevailed during America's greatest period of sustained growth), a Pareto distribution of income and wealth is the unsurprising and persistent outcome. While far from the only factor driving the current Pareto distribution of wealth in America, the historically low marginally effective tax rate on very high incomes has undoubtedly been a contributor to increasing inequality, and that contribution will continue.

Policy makers simply must increase the tax rates at the high end of incomes. Since 1987, at the federal level, the top marginal personal-income-tax rate has been below 40 percent and has averaged 36 percent—in contrast to the half-century preceding 1987, during which the rate averaged 80 percent.[27] This is by no means an untried, experimental idea. It is an idea that was tested and that proved effective for this very country for a half a century. By how much and starting at what income level the progressive rate should rise is open to different theories and arguments. In addition, the approach is complicated by the great variance in state personal income tax rates. Those top rates vary from nil (in nine states) to 13.3 percent in California, and the population-weighted median (across the fifty states) is a top rate of 5 percent.[28] My recommendation is a top federal rate of 45 percent for incomes between $500 thousand and $5 million, 55 percent between $5 million and $1 million, and 65 percent above $10 million (implying median top combined rates, factoring in state income taxes, of 50 percent, 60 percent, and 70 percent, respectively). What is clear is that we have gone past the point of having logic or data support the notion that the current personal-income-tax structure is contributing positively to future prospects for American democratic capitalism.

Getting Started

Getting started will not be a trivial undertaking for political leaders, especially elected ones, given the powerful duopoly in which they currently operate. The easiest thing for them to do is continue along the current path to maintain the current comfortable duopoly—until it crashes cataclysmically. Hence, they should start with initiatives that don't make them feel too uncomfortable—

anything else they will reject as too painful. For example, taking on powerful Wall Street interests to fight short-termism might not be the best place to attempt to build momentum.

Getting close to the real citizens who are the target beneficiaries of legislation during the process of designing it, as GDS did on the GOV.UK initiative, may be more comfortable. Plus, it will have the beneficial side effect of helping political leaders empathize with and show greater compassion for the electorate, which will make the legislative ideas more compelling. In addition, it is probably not terribly intimidating to set expectations low, by indicating that initiatives won't be designed perfectly and will need to be tweaked to improve them after launch. Finally, attaching a requirement for periodic review to new legislative initiatives isn't a terrifyingly difficult thing to imagine.

If political leaders get their feet wet on these sorts of initiatives, they can dive into the more substantive trade, antitrust, and tax issues, possibly with encouragement from their electorate.

Chapter 8

An Agenda for Educators

Beth Grosso teaches fourth- and fifth-grade students at Central Elementary School in Hamilton, Ontario, Canada's equivalent of Pittsburgh as the country's historic steel capital. Central Elementary is a venerable institution, opened in 1853 as the first public school in Hamilton. It is housed in a grand, classical building with brown and gray stonework, featuring a tall central tower adorned with a beautiful clock. While the school population at inception was probably pretty homogeneous, it most certainly is not today. Its students, overall, speak at least thirty languages in their respective homes, and English is a second language for an overwhelming majority.

Grosso doesn't immediately look the part of a superstar teacher. She is a relatively soft-spoken fifty-three-year-old with short brown hair and glasses who likes to read, cook, and garden and is a self-described introvert. There is a hint of her "the glass is always half-full" attitude in the perpetual trace of a smile on her face.

Yet Grosso is venerated by her peers as a teacher who is uniquely successful with her students. And you can see just by looking at her classroom that she's different. Student desks are in arranged in a U-shape, facing the board, not in rows, and Grosso's desk is behind them, not in front. Student-generated work seems to cover every square inch of the walls.

Over time, she has come to be seen as a miracle worker. Just before the summer holidays, teachers get their class lists—a chance to preview their new students and maybe get some tips from the kids' current teachers on how best to teach them. A number of years ago, when other teachers saw Grosso's list, they said, "Good luck. You're going to have to change your expectations of what's possible in your classroom." Looking at her class list, she knew that many of these kids spent more time in the principal's office than in the classroom. They were the kids characterized as disrespectful by their current teachers, kids who fought at recess and who always made snippy remarks back to teachers. Nonetheless, by midyear, one would never have guessed that Grosso's charges had been the same ones their previous teachers had lamented. They worked cohesively and had made huge strides in their learning. The student pegged as the most troublesome and disruptive routinely offered to sweep Grosso's classroom floor rather than go outside for recess, and was under consideration for the most-improved award given at the end of the school year.

Of Fish, Hamsters, and Snowballs

While Grosso understands that part of her official job is to transmit a body of content from her head to those of the students, she thinks her real job—her most important job—is to help students become capable of thinking in a complex and uncertain world. To her that means embracing the messiness of the world and not attempting to simplify it for students as if students can't deal with messiness.

That means helping them learn both how to build models (rather than handing them prebuilt ones) and how to build better ones together. She introduces them to the ladder of inference, a framework from business and education theorist Chris Argyris, which describes how humans reason, starting with selecting which data to take into account and then making increasingly specific inferences about the selected data—up the rungs of a metaphoric ladder to reach a conclusion on the subject of their thinking, at the top of that ladder. Grosso creates an exercise by which she writes different fragments of a story on a number of paper fish that she hides around the classroom. For example, the story may be about why she arrived at school grumpy one morning, and one fish may say "woke up late" while another may say "forgot marked tests at home," and so on. Student groups go on a fishing expedition to find and collect the fish, and then attempt to come to a conclusion based on the fish that their group happened to find.

Since different groups find different data-laden fish, the groups come to different conclusions. Instead of judging which conclusion is "right," they explore how collecting different data means that each group might come to a different conclusion. Grosso highlights that although we can never collect all the data ourselves, we make our model more robust by being curious and asking questions of others who may have access to data that we don't. By rejecting the need for one "right" answer, Grosso's students become more confident. They gain the confidence to share their thinking, because if their answer is different from others', it might just be because they collected different data or interpreted the data differently, not because their answer is "wrong." The process also encourages students to make and think about connections—between what they and other students know—so that they can integrate multiple insights.

While Grosso's expectations are high, sometimes her students still surprise their teacher. In a lesson on personal responsibility, Grosso read them a story about a kid who took a pet hamster to school against the wishes of his mother, and the hamster got out of his backpack and ran around the school causing problems. The exercise for the students was to submit their opinion on whether the kid was acting responsibly or not, and provide their reasoning. With one exception, the students declared the kid to be irresponsible, because he hadn't listened to his mother and that led to him causing a problem at the school. But one student saw the situation differently. Drawing from his own life, in which his older brother had recently bought a snake as a pet, the singular student reasoned that the kid worried that when everybody was out of the house, something unfortunate would happen to the hamster—like being eaten by a snake. So, he was showing highly responsible care for the hamster. That wasn't an answer Grosso was expecting, but she knew she shouldn't and couldn't mark it wrong. Instead, it presented a fabulous learning opportunity for the students on the power of diversity in models of the same situation.

A student once expressed the power of building broad models to Grosso in a way that she found endearing and unforgettable: "Ideas are like snowballs. When you roll it with other ideas, it gets bigger. A snowball doesn't discriminate. It doesn't say yes to some snowflakes and no to other snowflakes. It picks up all the snowflakes in its path and it just keeps going and going, until finally, you can make a snowman." And this, essentially, is what a natural system is: not just a collection of snowflakes but something in its own right—a snowman.

Grosso also teaches her students not to fear failure, because, as she puts it, "It's in failing that the kids learn. You stand back watching, and thinking it's not going to be pretty, but I want to see them muck about, because if I'm always there giving them the answers, they're not going to learn to be problem solvers in life."[1] To help them learn about failure and how, when necessary, to go back to the drawing board to come up with better answers, she lets them choose a project to work on every year.

Nearly all of them had been enrolled in English-as-a-second-language (ESL) classes earlier in their schooling, so one year they chose to work on finding a better way to deliver ESL to students in the younger grades. They came up with a plan, which Grosso knew was not going to succeed. But rather than telling them this, she just encouraged them test out their thinking with the ESL teacher and the targeted students before doing too much planning. They did, and came back realizing that their plan wouldn't work. But rather than admonishing them for doing a bad job, Grosso encouraged them to take the feedback, tear down what wasn't going to fly, and then build on the pieces that were looking better. They eventually came up with a better plan and did helpful ESL work. But that wasn't the important outcome. It was learning how to build and test and rebuild and test and rebuild again—with the attendant rewards at the end of the process.

Beth Grosso's approach underlies the agenda I propose here for educators to help preserve American democratic capitalism and enhance its ability to sustainably deliver broadening and rising prosperity. The job of educators should be to prepare students for a complex adaptive system, not to make them capable of operating only a narrow part of a complicated machine. We need to equip our youth for a world that isn't about perfecting a machine but rather about achieving a balance—an endless journey of transitory improvements rather than definitive solutions. That is the only way we will produce the citizens that we need and the business executives and political leaders to pilot productively. Currently, the formal education system produces overconfident reductionists who don't see that they are operating in a complex adaptive system and are altogether too sure of the quality and usability of their piece-part solutions. The purpose of education needs to shift, as Beth Grosso illustrates, toward producing sophisticated yet humble model integrators. To do so, educators must do four things.

Temper the Inclination to Teach Certainty

At present, the formal education system predominantly teaches certainty; that is, that there is one right answer and many wrong ones. This is instantiated in the standardized tests that govern to which higher-educational institutions one is given access: the SAT, ACT, GRE, MCAT, LSAT, GMAT. Their form could not be clearer. The majority of each test is composed of multiple-choice questions, each of which features three or four wrong answers and one right answer. If you can figure out which is which on a consistent basis, you will be admitted to the educational institution of your choice. If not, you are out of luck. There is zero reward for nuance, for "maybes," for "it depends."

There are certainly some right answers—like how many planets there are in our solar system: nine, at least until Pluto was downgraded to a dwarf planet and lumped together with lots of other dwarf planets. And while we're on the subject, was that downgrade legitimate or should Pluto still be a planet?[2] As with the planethood of Pluto, the vast majority of answers aren't *certainly* right. They are merely the best interpretation we have yet come up with, just as Newton's law of universal gravitation was the best interpretation when he conceived of it. But it wasn't "right." It was just the best available and is now viewed more properly, thanks to Einstein, as mostly but not always right. Yet Newton's law of universal gravitation was taught as the absolute truth from the late seventeenth century to the early/mid twentieth century, when general relativity began being widely taught.

Despite humanity's long and painful history of being shown to be wrong about what was previously held to be certain, we keep teaching models as if they are not models but rather reality—the true unshakeable reality, rather than what they are: the best interpretation of reality humanity has been able to come up with yet.

Instead, we need to teach students—at all levels—that all models are wrong, otherwise they wouldn't be models in the first place. Rather than teaching students to uncritically adopt models, with all their implicit flaws, we need to teach students how to critically evaluate models. Even more important, we need to teach students how to build new ones. That is what human advancement is about: building better models. But only in the rarified air of PhD programs is model building a core aspect of the educational experience. The rest of the educational sphere is primarily concerned with learning and applying the existing models of the world—as if they were certainly correct.

This most definitely does not need to be the case. Students don't need to wait until they enter a PhD program—which only a distinct minority of undergraduates ever ends up doing—to engage in mental model building. Beth Grosso demonstrates that her fourth- and fifth-grade students can easily learn to build new models and challenge existing ones. And it goes further still: children as young as kindergarten-aged can be taught to reflect on how they model and to build new models by taking into account differing views. Some observers worry that being taught that there typically is no right answer will make kids indecisive or confused. In fact, the opposite occurs: they become more confident in thinking their way through a complex and uncertain world.

This is a key insight from the I-Think initiative, which was incubated at the Rotman School of Management and is now a freestanding nonprofit educational organization.[3] Founded in 2009 under the leadership of Ellie Avishai (then led by Jennifer Riel, and now Josie Fung), the initiative began working with secondary-school teachers and students because it assumed at the time that elementary-school students would not yet have developed the metacognitive skills to tackle reflecting on and building models. That turned out to be a flawed and pessimistic assumption, as elementary teachers who had come to I-Think teacher-training programs, including Beth Grosso, began teaching the tools and techniques to younger and younger students—all the way to kindergarten students—with great success.

The I-Think initiative helps teachers assist K–12 students to learn to be better problem solvers. The approach makes students more cognizant of what data they select to use as a basis for their reasoning and what data they choose to ignore or discount. It further helps them understand that others may be exposed to different data, or may prioritize their data differently, as with Grosso and her fish. The methodology then assists them in reflecting on and being more conscious of how they interpret the data to form their own model of what they think is operative. Also, it encourages students to expect that others with whom they work will utilize nonoverlapping data, will arrive at different interpretations of the same data, and will as often as not create different models. Because of that understanding, students are more likely to be curious about models that differ from their own, and are more likely to be enthusiastic about working with those whose models differ, in order to build models that are superior to the ones each began with.

Rather than learning that they should strive for certainty in an inherently uncertain world, I-Think students learn a methodology for getting to better models than they start out with, by using alternative models, alternative interpretations, and alternative data to build them. Their teachers find that the collaborative, critical-thinking, and creative skills of their students jump off the proverbial charts when the goal of *certainty* is replaced with the goal of *reflectiveness*.

It goes almost without saying that if K–12 students can learn a productive alternative to obsessing about certainty, then college and university students should be able to do so with ease. That is and is not the case. Intellectually the older students are easily prepared. However, by the time they have gotten to university, they are typically so obsessed with certainty that they are less open to learning than their K–12 counterparts are—a tricky challenge, and one that suggests that early education is superior to waiting until the students are "old enough."

Stop Teaching Reductionism as If It Is a Good Thing

Throughout the education system, we teach that reductionism is a laudable activity, is the right thing to do. For the vast majority of subjects and in the vast majority of times, students are taught each subject as if the others don't exist in space or time. When things get messy, we hold all else equal to reduce the problem in question to parts we can more easily deal with.

We have already seen numerous examples of that in this book. Performance management (i.e., providing compensation incentives for meeting goals) is completely divorced from the process of setting the goals in question. Determination of an "optimal financial structure" is considered apart from the question of how managers behave when working under a crushing debt load. Zero-based budgeting is performed without consideration of how consumers make their purchase decisions. Typically, the people making these narrow but inherently connected decisions work in different departments and, despite the critical interrelationships among the domains, have no interaction with each other during the process of making their decisions.

The drawback with this approach is that we stop questioning whether the breakdown of the problem we're about to tackle is appropriate, and we don't look at evidence suggesting that broader approaches might work better for a given problem. We're handed a toolbox of generic and narrow problem-solving methods along with instructions on when and how to use them, and learning consists of practicing the applications of these methods. We're not actually taught how to figure out how to solve problems.

Current educational approaches discourage integration across different disciplines. It's not hard to see why: teaching a single discipline and its models is much easier for the instructor than having to talk about other disciplines and making connections to them. Besides, having been trained themselves in single disciplines, few are going to comfortably make the leap to a more integrative approach to teaching. In our education system we essentially teach sets of independent certainties to young students in the hope that they'll make any links they need to on their own and determine the right approach to any given problem by themselves. Sadly, few students figure out how to create those integrative solutions. Most are overwhelmed and never even try. Instead they come to view the world as a mysterious place in which they attempt to survive as best they can, rather than a friendlier place that they can engage with at least a modicum of confidence.

To compound the problem, teaching is a closed loop. Current educators were taught to honor reductionism by a previous generation of reductionist educators, who were taught by a previous generation still, and they teach the only thing they know—reductionism—to their students, some of whom go on to become educators and repeat the only cycle that they have ever experienced.

This may all sound like a caricature, but it is a pretty faithful description of modern management education—about which I do know a thing or two from a long career as dean of a business school. The flagship business degree is the master's in business administration (MBA), which has grown to a fifth of all graduate degrees given out in America each year.[4] Despite management guru Peter Drucker's admonition that in business there are actually no decisions that fit nicely into narrow specialties, I will attest on oath to any congressional committee that teaching in MBA programs is structured around narrowly based disciplines, like finance, accounting, marketing, production operations, and human resources, and that within each course, teachers identify a standard set of problems, which they then teach students how to solve.

That was not how it was supposed to be. When Harvard Business School (HBS) opened its doors in 1908 to offer the world's first MBA, it was supposed to teach "general management." Its flagship course on that integrative subject, business policy, debuted in 1912.[5] When I entered the HBS MBA program sixty-seven years later, in the fall of 1979, all my courses were in narrow disciplines, with little or no attempt made by professors to relate them to one another, with the exception (supposedly) of the venerable business-policy course, the first half of which was in the final group of courses offered in first year and the second half of which was the only required course in the second year.

I waited with bated breath for the signature course that would pull together my first-year learning and set me up for my second year. However, I was sadly disappointed. The entire content of business policy was an admonition for top managers to make good decisions because they were good, and avoid bad ones because they were bad. That was it. There was not a shred of usable content in the entire course. The message was clear. HBS thinks a lot about narrow disciplinary knowledge, so there is massive content infused in the narrow disciplinary courses. But it doesn't think about integrative business knowledge, so in business policy there is literally no content.

Business academics have proven to be quite adept at dealing with threats from integrative approaches. When business strategy became an important idea in the 1960s and fueled the growth of a new class of advisory firm, the strategy-consulting firms, starting with Boston Consulting Group and then Bain & Company, business schools added courses in strategy to their curricula. Strategy started off with the promise of showing how the disciplines are pulled together to make interdisciplinary choices. But that was a threat to the disciplines, and over the years, somehow, they put strategy into a box. It became itself a narrow discipline, with its courses designed to fit beside marketing, finance, accounting, etc., and to teach a toolbox of narrow analytical strategy concepts and techniques.

After my disappointment with business policy, I hoped that I would see an evolution toward more-integrative business education. But it evolved in the opposite direction, toward more-narrow specialization and reductionism. Seeing the gap when I became dean of the Rotman School of Management in 1998, I decided to work on content that we could teach for thinking across the narrow disciplines that we taught. In 2005, we started teaching integrative thinking, which was a technique for taking the prescriptions from two different disciplinary models and determining how to make an interdisciplinary decision that factored in the two models but didn't simply adopt one at the expense of the other. The methodology generalized over time to deal with conflicting models, whether they came from the traditional narrow business disciplines or any other siloed environment.

Integrative thinking at Rotman demonstrates that reductionism can be countered and integration taught.[6] Other schools picked up on and are teaching variants of integrative-thinking concepts pioneered at Rotman. However, it was a difficult slog against the reductionist disciplinary habits and practices in the business academy. It was, in short, the hardest thing I have ever attempted.

That is just an example from business education. Others have taken to heart that if we know that students will graduate into and live in a complex adaptive system, we should teach students explicitly about how those systems work and how to make decisions that are consistent with them. MIT, for example, has a long history of teaching students about complexity. The late professor Jay Forrester pioneered the concept of system dynamics at MIT in the 1950s. He is also famous for being the father of random-access memory (RAM), which was instrumental in the evolution of computers.[7] Since his time, MIT students (especially at the Sloan School of Management, where Forrester spent the greatest part of his MIT career) have been taught how complex systems work and the challenges they present. His student and protégé John Sterman (mentioned in chapter 1 and elsewhere) now holds the Jay W. Forrester Professorship and serves as director of the System Dynamics Group. The group not only teaches MIT students about complex adaptive systems, it makes case studies and teaching materials available under a creative-commons license online in its LearningEdge platform so that educators around the world can gain the ability to teach about complex adaptive systems at no cost.

Some years later, in 1984, under the leadership of, among others, Manhattan Project veteran and Los Alamos National Laboratory senior scientist George Cowan, the Santa Fe Institute opened its doors.[8] It has been dedicated to the multidisciplinary study of complex adaptive systems since its inception. In addition to doing research to better understand complex adaptive systems, it offers a variety of educational programs on the subject. More recently still, in 1996, the New England Complex Systems Institute was founded and, like the Santa Fe Institute, offers courses to the public and educators in addition to carrying out academic research.[9]

On the one hand, it is fortunate that there are plenty of resources available to teach students of all ages about the functioning of complex adaptive systems. On the other hand, it is unfortunate that only a small percentage of today's students get to benefit from such learning. For the complex adaptive system that we know as American democratic capitalism to have a stronger future, the educational footprint of complex adaptive systems has to expand. Educators across fields need to break out of the closed loop and teach the merits of integrating as broadly as our minds are capable of doing. Why? Because the instant those students step outside the walls of the classroom, they're faced with a complex adaptive system that doesn't follow the rules of reductionism. Instead, it is characterized by connections that need to be understood and managed carefully and continuously if the system is to survive the adaptive behavior of the agents operating within its different parts. That world needs and demands integrative solutions that students are currently ill-prepared to provide. Any movement, however small, toward less reductionism and more integrative thinking in the students' education is an important step in the right direction.

Help Students Appreciate the Power of Directly Observable Data

To improve the quality of their models, students need to be taught to interact more closely with the real world. The closer to the real world you get, the better grounded your models of it will be. This was the insight of the aforementioned Chris Argyris. He distinguished between "directly observable data" and the kind of interpretations observers will make about the data.[10] With regard to the former, multiple people observing will see it as the same (or at least similar) data. For example, all drivers who stop at the scene of a car accident would probably agree that there is an unconscious lady at the wheel of her car. However, there would probably be as many interpretations of what caused the accident as there are observers: "I bet she fell asleep at the wheel." "Another car must have cut her off, because she looks like a responsible driver." "They don't police speeding drivers on this highway: she was probably driving too fast."

Theorizing is important. It is what we do to make sense of the world around us and build models for taking action. But theorizing on the back of someone else's interpretations is never going to be as powerful as theorizing on the basis of your own interpretations of real interactions with your subject—whatever that subject happens to be.

If we want students to build more-effective models of their world in order to be able to design more-useful action, we need to help them learn how to access more directly observable data on that world. Otherwise, they will default to using interpretations of somebody else's directly observable data. The best way to do that is to teach students the basics of ethnography, the qualitative study of individuals and cultural groups. Rather than teaching students that data is restricted to numbers that appear mysteriously for the student to analyze, or teaching the accumulation of quantitative data via arms-length surveys, educators need to teach students that data, both qualitative and quantitative, gleaned from watching real people engage in real activities, is the most powerful tool for building better models for how the world works. Those models can be tested quantitatively to refine them. But the attempt to build models of our complex adaptive world purely on the basis of quantitative analysis of data will lead to narrow reductionism and irrelevance.

The Hasso Plattner Institute of Design at Stanford, colloquially known as the d.school, provides an example of successfully teaching ethnography at scale. The d.school got its start when Plattner, the cofounder of German software giant SAP, read the cover story of the May 17, 2004, issue of *BusinessWeek*, featuring the design firm IDEO.[11] He was compelled by the article to phone up David Kelley, the cofounder of IDEO, who was pictured on the cover, to offer him $35 million in funding to create an educational program to teach the tools and techniques that were discussed in the article.[12] That educational program became the d.school, which was founded in 2005.

The d.school teaches "design thinking," which includes rigorous ethnographic methods for gaining deep understanding of users. It is an understatement to say that the d.school has been wildly successful. It has become a signature feature of the Stanford educational landscape in only a decade and a half. Students from across the campus—not just business and engineering—vie for seats in its classes. Every year, thousands of corporate executives, nonprofit managers, Stanford students, and educators from K–12 through graduate schools attend its various programs.

Thanks to leaders like the d.school but also to the IIT Institute of Design, at the Illinois Institute of Technology, most design schools in the country teach ethnographic approaches to deep user understanding. Also, engineering programs are increasingly teaching user-experience (UX) design as part of their core curricula and many schools now feature degree programs in UX design. Business schools are getting better at including courses on design/ethnography/deep user understanding. Rotman (University of Toronto) was considered a leader when it started teaching design thinking in 2006.[13] Schools such as Darden (University of Virginia) and Weatherhead (Case Western) were early adherents as well, and now many leading business schools feature design-thinking courses or programs, including MIT/Sloan, Harvard Business School, Columbia, and Cornell.[14] However, very few of these courses or programs are taught by full-time tenure-stream faculty, so design thinking/ethnography/deep user understanding are still fringe subjects at business schools across the country. But at least the material is available to students.

Regrettably, schools of public policy for the most part lag behind in this domain. A review of twelve top schools of public policy shows zero required courses featuring ethnography.[15] Only two of the schools, Harvard's Kennedy School and NYU's Wagner School, feature an elective course on the subject, and in both cases it is a single course. Clearly, getting close to the user is not high on the agenda in this field.

While progress is being made on teaching students the tools and techniques for getting closer to the real world in order to inform decisions, more needs to be done. K–12 educators can follow the lead of Beth Grosso (and educators who work with I-Think) in guiding students in that direction. Those educating future business executives and public-policy makers need to make deep user understanding and ethnographic approaches more central to their research and curricula, especially the schools of public policy.

Elevate the Appreciation of Qualities

As the world has gotten more science driven and data obsessed, the formal educational system is teaching certainty with ever more confidence. The message being transmitted to students is, crunch the data and you can determine "the truth." And we wonder why political positions have become more entrenched! Instead we need to inculcate a belief in the benefits of balancing the manipulation of quantities with the appreciation of qualities.[16] Because science requires numeric quantities and mathematical methods for manipulating those quantities to determine "the truth," we intensively teach the manipulation of quantities—starting with addition, then subtraction, then multiplication, then division, then algebra, then calculus, etc. This causes our students to become highly experienced and skilled in seeking out quantifiable variables and crunching data so as to determine "the truth."

However, many very important things in life cannot be quantified—the strength of one's love, happiness, the beauty of an object, the quality of one's life, the merit of an economy, etc. They have qualities that can't be quantified but can be appreciated. Very little in our formal education system helps students become skilled in the appreciation of qualities. It happens in literature, fine-arts, and design courses, in which students are helped to make finer and finer distinctions in the qualitative attributes of their subject matter. But those fields are now a tiny portion of the formal educational world—only 8 percent of all university graduates annually now major in the humanities broadly defined.[17] Development of appreciation of qualities happens only rarely, and sometimes not at all, in the teaching of the natural sciences and most of the social sciences.

As a consequence, we produce students who systematically lack balance. They are strong in the manipulation of quantities and weak in the appreciation of qualities. They are overly certain of the correctness of their models and their analyses based on those models and are equally certain of the incorrectness of opposing points of view. They are confident that they have looked at all data that is relevant to a position and that other variables, by definition, are not at all relevant.

We need to arrest these tendencies. We need to teach students to balance the manipulation of quantities with the appreciation of qualities. We need to teach them that their conclusions are interpretations, not fact or truth, and that alternative interpretations might be equally meritorious and/or contribute to generating a still more meritorious interpretation. That is the only way they will be prepared to work productively in a complex adaptive system.

Greater balance will increase the probability that future executives will look beyond the simplest numbers to determine what decision is right for their business. It will also encourage future citizens to push their elected officials and the companies for which they (the citizens) work and from whom they buy goods and services to come up with more-productive solutions. Maybe it will even cause future members of Congress to actually want to work together to generate better solutions for the country rather than vowing never to work with the terrible people on the other side of the aisle—who are so clearly wrong!

This balance is anything but a new or novel concept. It is a core idea in both Eastern and Western philosophy, stemming from the same era—the fourth century BC. In China, philosopher Zou

Yan (305 BC–240 BC) is generally credited with the creation of the philosophy of yin and yang, which argues for harmony between the human forces of yin (soft, receiving, accepting, humble, calm) and yang (hard, giving, motivated, joyful, energetic).[18] The school of thought views the two forces in human nature as complementary and interdependent. The philosophy considers it, at best, counterproductive to focus on developing the qualities of one to the exclusion of the other—at worst, downright impossible.

Meanwhile, in Greece, Aristotle (384 BC–322 BC) argued for the pursuit of the golden mean in his seminal work, *Nicomachean Ethics*. To Aristotle, the extremes are vices and the mean represents virtue. For example, undue humility and empty vanity are opposing vices at the extremes and proper pride is the virtue at the golden mean between them. Cowardice and recklessness are vices, while courage is the virtue. According to Aristotle, achieving the golden mean is challenging. It is neither an arithmetic average of the extremes nor the same in every situation. Each context requires its own attempt to find the virtuous mean. However, the individual who strives consistently to achieve the golden mean will be a happy and virtuous person, according to Aristotle's philosophy.[19]

The value of balance has been accepted as essential to human harmony and effectiveness in both Eastern and Western thought for over two millennia. Arguably, thanks to the centrality of yin and yang to the Taoist school of thought, the pursuit of balance has been nurtured, in thought and practice, more in Eastern philosophy than in Western philosophy, which is perhaps why education in America does not embrace or teach Aristotle's golden mean to any major extent. But it is there for the taking. Balance has been taught, and the literature and pedagogy are available to any educator committed to teaching balance rather than extremes.

Some educational institutions are taking up the challenge. University education in the United Kingdom has long been the home of highly specialized disciplines that require secondary-school specialization (in the A-levels) to even apply. That history notwithstanding, Bristol University now offers an undergraduate degree in anthropology with innovation, a degree that promises to "bring together arts, science, engineering, humanities and enterprise to deliver innovative products, services and ways of living."[20] Massachusetts Institute of Technology, historically America's preeminent science and technology university, now offers a bachelor of science in humanities and science, which promises that it "draws from both humanistic and scientific studies, providing students with a basic command of each mode of inquiry."[21] These programs may or may not deliver entirely on their promises, but it is encouraging to see that they make an attempt at teaching the critical balance.

Getting Started

Many educators reading this will argue that they already do the four things suggested above. They don't teach certainty. They are reductionist only to the extent that is appropriate and necessary. They teach about directly observable data. And they teach qualitative appreciation. That may be true in their particular cases. I have no way of knowing and no intention of arguing with them. But the sum of all education in America is woefully deficient across these areas. If every educator just started leaning a little bit more from where they are today in the direction of the four themes described in this chapter, democratic capitalism would have a brighter future.

The best way for educators to start is to teach something in which they already have some background. For most, that does not include complex adaptive systems or integrating across knowledge domains. The starting point should be tempering the inclination to teach certainty. In general, educators have learned how the models in their domain have changed and advanced over time. They can teach that history to students to illustrate that students shouldn't assume that the current model educators are teaching is certain or correct. Rather it is the latest in a long series of mankind's advancements on the issue in question, advancements that will likely continue.

That will lead in the direction of students internalizing the idea that they can and should be a part of the critical study and advancement of the models in use around them, not just users of those models. That doesn't need to wait until they are in university or even secondary school. The earlier the start, the better. Leading students toward the path of achieving more-productive balance in their views cannot start too early.

Chapter 9

An Agenda for Citizens

The Leamington Ketchup Affair

In 2016 a serious dustup occurred in Canada, spurred by consumers outraged over, of all things, the location of ketchup production. The story began in February 2013, when 3G Capital (mentioned in chapter 6) took control of Heinz, the world's dominant ketchup maker. Nine months later, in November 2013, in the midst of a major global cost-cutting campaign, the company informed workers in its Leamington plant, located in the heart of vegetable-farming country in southwestern Ontario, that the facility would be closing in June 2014 and ketchup production moved to the United States.

Leamington's payroll included 749 full-time employees and 350 seasonal workers, and the facility consumed approximately half of the tomatoes grown annually in Ontario. That meant that all Heinz ketchup sold in Canada would thereafter be produced in the United States and made from American-grown tomatoes. That was a big deal, because approximately 84 percent of the ketchup sold in Canada was Heinz ketchup.[1]

The plant workers and farmers were voluble in their protests from the start, but their objections seemed to fall on deaf ears. But one very important pair of ears did pick up the message and decided to act on the information. In December 2015, a year and a half after Leamington shut down, the world's biggest mustard producer, French's, then a subsidiary of UK giant Reckitt Benckiser Group PLC, launched a ketchup into the Canadian market, loudly proclaiming that its product was made entirely with Canadian tomatoes.

Canadian consumers had clearly been waiting for this. A Facebook post by Brian Fernandez on February 23, 2016, extolling the virtues of French's Canadian ketchup, went viral, earning a quarter of a million shares and making a trend of the hashtag #Frenchsketchup. Despite the positive publicity, the initial sales of the new ketchup brand were not sufficiently impressive for Canada's biggest grocery chain, Loblaws, which commands a 34 percent grocery-market share. In March 2016, Loblaws announced that it was dropping French's ketchup.[2] But the decision triggered such an intense consumer outcry that Loblaws reversed course completely within days and announced it was restocking French's ketchup across its entire chain. "We've heard our Loblaws customers. We will restock French's ketchup and hope that the enthusiasm we are seeing in the media and on social media translates into sales of the product," said Kevin Groh, Loblaws vice president of corporate affairs and communication.[3]

For his part, French's president, Elliott Penner, was overwhelmed by the consumer support his company received in Canada: "We've done this for a long time, and I don't think I've ever seen a public outcry like this before. It really shows you how much power consumers have when they want to be heard, and they've been heard. We'll always be indebted to them for that."[4] French's responded to this consumer support by beginning in 2017 to bottle its ketchup in Canada, so that the ketchup wasn't just made with Canadian tomatoes. The company thereby provided its loyal Canadian consumers a 100 percent Canadian-made product. By the end of 2018, French's had achieved a market share of about 5 percent, accounting for most of the 6 percentage point decline in Heinz's share (from 84 percent down to 78 percent).

Citizens were deploying their purchasing power using a technique, the buycott, that is a cousin of the venerable tactic of boycotting, a form of protest made famous in America by the 1955 African American boycott of the Montgomery Bus Line. A year later, the state law that actually required segregated seating on buses was declared unconstitutional.[5] The buycott is the obverse of the boycott. It involves consumers buying more from a given producer in order to reward behavior. Canadian consumers weren't actually attempting to stop Heinz in its tracks or cause it to reopen Leamington—the typical kinds of goals of boycotts. They just wanted to reward French's for behavior that they liked.

This story illustrates how individual citizens can work to restore balance to the economy. By choosing to buy ketchup from a less dominant supplier, consumers were able to mitigate the effects of Heinz's efficiency drive on the resilience of that part of the Canadian economy—thus reinforcing resilience at the expense of efficiency. Without consumer support, an alternative supplier would not have spotted an opportunity. By enabling a credible competitor to gain a foothold in this market, the buycott has made it less of a monoculture dependent on a single, potentially abusive player. Having Heinz produce and sell virtually all the ketchup in Canada may have been efficient, and the availability of alternative ketchups may not have been so important to consumers. But having alternative buyers for their produce was certainly important for Canadian tomato growers, which Canadian citizens clearly realized.

Citizens will need to make more of these sorts of contributions if they are to play their part in saving democratic capitalism. Without citizen push, political leaders won't put the requisite effort into solving the key problems and neither will business executives. Citizens have responsibility for playing a more central role, for pushing governments and businesses to act. This will necessitate citizens recognizing that they have a key role in shaping the complex adaptive system of which they are a part. They need to push for limits on efficiency, because political and business leaders won't—or won't be able to—do much without that support.

There are four core ways in which citizens can accomplish this agenda: They can utilize their purchasing power, leverage collective action, insist on reciprocal political relationships, and make each vote count. For each I will give examples of citizens doing this already. These initiatives aren't new to the world. They just aren't practiced widely enough.

Utilize Their Purchasing Power

The French's ketchup buycott case above is just one example of what citizens can do when they pool their purchasing power. Citizens, in their capacity as buyers, need to use that power to introduce friction into markets that otherwise have too little. Such friction helps stem the tide toward a Pareto distribution of the benefits to be had from the operation of highly efficient production machines.

When citizen-consumers don't ask whether the good or service they are buying was produced by workers earning a living wage, while working in a safe environment, the consumers are propping up unsustainable businesses at home (such as many large American retailers, whose low wages and unstable work schedules make it hard for their floor-level workers to meet basic health, food, housing, and childcare needs) and contributing to the exporting of jobs to jurisdictions with unsafe working conditions.

It is encouraging, therefore, that an infrastructure is developing to facilitate buycotts like that of French's. There now exists, for example, a web platform, www.buycott.com, that facilitates the scanning of Universal Product Codes (UPCs) to reveal pertinent facts about a product.[6] These facts then allow consumers to make a more informed decision as to whether they should purchase an item or seek an alternative produced with more-laudable practices. Buycott.com also lists a number of buycott campaigns that consumers can join. The platform is an example of how consumers, without having to do anything more than scan a barcode with their phone, can push back and take loosely organized collective action.

The buycott, though, is an attempt to fix a problem that has already appeared. It would be better to prevent the problem in the first place, which requires a less dramatic but no less important change in behavior. When citizens default, as they often do, to using the leading provider of a particular good or service, they are contributing to Pareto outcomes: monopolization and monocultures. Unfortunately, it is very tempting for consumers—arguably efficient for them—to focus on a single, familiar provider. Switching to an alternative can be painful and annoying. And there are, of course, the much discussed network effects in the modern economy. It makes lots of sense to use Facebook for your social networking, because everybody else with whom you would like to network is on Facebook, or to pick Instagram over Snapchat, because Instagram is integrated with its giant social-media owner, Facebook.

These network effects are not just found in the online world. There is a benefit to you of buying the leading brand in categories like beer, laundry detergents, and athletic shoes, because the leading brand is most likely to be in stock at whatever retailers you visit (whether physical or online). And thanks to its leading scale, it often has the best cost position, enabling it to deliver superior value for you, the consumer. So, the effect (leading) becomes the cause of more of that effect (leading more so) and so on. And as has been discussed, that is the road to a Pareto distribution.

Citizens can combat this powerful tendency through what is called multihoming.[7] Rather than dedicating their purchasing power to one provider of a given product or service, citizen-consumers can split their purchases. They can take Uber sometimes, Lyft others, and taxis still others. They can get some of their news through their Facebook feed and still subscribe to their local newspaper. They can use Facebook for some things but rather than use Facebook subsidiary Instagram for their photo sharing, use Instagram rival Snapchat. They can buy some things from Amazon Prime and others from their local retailer. The natural tendency is the opposite—and that is why we are seeing so many distributions tending toward Pareto. The effect (using Uber or Facebook or Amazon) becomes the cause of more of the effect (using Uber or Facebook or Amazon even more). Multihoming puts helpful friction into the effect–cause–effect sequence, restoring balance between efficiency and resilience.

Multihoming and buycotts are two techniques by which citizens can use their purchasing power to produce better outcomes for democratic capitalism. But there is opportunity to double down in utilizing that purchasing power to thwart monopolization and build redundancy and resilience.

Leverage Collective Action

A buycott is one form of collective action. But citizens can leverage collective action more broadly to build in productive redundancy in the face of political inaction. Collective action is, of course, "old school," exemplified by Martin Luther King Jr. and the civil-rights movement, Cesar Chavez and agricultural-worker unionization, and the Love Canal families and the creation of the Environmental Protection Agency's Superfund. Old fashioned though it may seem, collective action is an important and underutilized countervailing force against both a winner-take-all marketplace and Washington's duopoly grip on legislation and regulation.

As sociologist Charles Tilly pointed out in 1993, collective actions can be multiplicatively powerful: numbers × commitment × unity × worthiness.[8] This formula worked when Cesar Chavez endeavored to organize agricultural workers in 1965. He had large numbers of workers who had high commitment. He drove unity, and it was viewed as a sufficiently worthy cause. When he organized a consumer boycott of grapes, consumers backed the large numbers of committed, united, and worthy workers until such time as his workers were able to unionize for the first time.

Customers in buying groups can create countervailing scale against giant companies. AARP, for instance, already utilizes this technique to negotiate better deals for its members with giant companies. More recently, consumer boycotts forced Sea-World Entertainment to end orca breeding programs and phase orca-based shows out of its repertoire within a specified time and compelled Nestlé to commit to a zero-deforestation policy in its palm-oil supply chain.[9] In an increasingly Pareto world, citizens need to be prepared to use collective action combined with their purchasing power to ameliorate Pareto outcomes.

Collective action can also be used as a redundant force against the power of duopoly legislators. Non-politically-aligned movements like Mothers Against Drunk Driving (MADD) can successfully tackle issues that politicians won't take on, because were it not for a group like MADD, it would be more convenient for politicians to do nothing than to expend time and resources attempting to catalyze action.

MADD was founded in 1980 after Candace Lightner's thirteen-year-old daughter, Cari, was killed by a drunk driver who had been released from jail only two days earlier and had four previous drunk-driving arrests. Lightner soon joined with relatives of other drunk-driving victims to found MADD. MADD added chapters rapidly, and after less than a year had already received $160,000 in donations and public funding. The movement achieved early success with federal action in 1984 to raise state drinking ages to twenty-one years.[10]

MADD retains its grassroots identity by combining activist local chapters with a board of directors heavily involved in management. A strong central bureaucracy is responsible for administration, freeing up the MADD national president (historically a relative of a drunk-driving victim) to serve as the organization's chief spokesperson. "Victim-activists" in MADD are aided by experts in traffic safety, lobbying, media, and fundraising in order to maximize the organization's impact. In addition, MADD provides extensive victim services to relatives of drunk-driving incidents, which has proved to be a fertile recruiting ground for MADD members.[11]

Let's see how MADD scores in terms of Charles Tilly's formula.

Numbers. In 2015, 98 percent of Americans reported that they view drunk driving as a very or somewhat serious problem, although this view is weaker among older Americans. This reflects the effect of MADD's educational campaigns, and the fact that anti-drunk-driving views were not as prevalent when MADD was founded.[12] In its early years MADD gained support and new members by redefining the victims of drunk driving as all family and friends of those involved in the car crash. This served to expand the number of people who could publicly identify and arouse sympathy as victims.[13] MADD's activism has raised support for restrictive drunk-driving laws, support even among older Americans, to levels that are impossible for lawmakers to ignore.

Commitment. MADD members are strongly committed to their cause, likely because most are victim-activists whose involvement was triggered by personal tragedy.[14] In addition, from its start MADD received substantial government technical and lobbying assistance that made it easier to stay committed to the cause. Finally, MADD has advocated a virtuous cause with little forceful opposition.[15]

Unity. MADD has been able to maintain strong unity within its movement through robust organization. MADD is a top-down organization with strict control over membership requirements and recognition of local chapters. However, these chapters remain involved in high-level policy discussions and their representatives make up a majority of the national board of directors. It has been important for chapters of MADD to be able to operate independently at the local level, with distinct agendas in some cases. Since most drunk-driving legislation is at the state level, it is essential that state chapters are all broadly on the same message but nimble enough to adjust individual activist agendas to take advantage of local opportunities.[16]

Worthiness. Worthiness has been extremely important for MADD. This is clear in the important role assigned to victims of drunk driving, who give a persuasive human face to MADD. As victims, these individuals are "perceived to have a legitimate grievance" by MADD's audience. In fact, a quantitative study of state-level organizations' ability to raise state drinking ages to twenty-one shows that the most important organizational characteristics were related to legitimacy (e.g., the chapter president's victim status and the percentage of victim membership), even more than the organization's age, membership size, and financial resources.[17] MADD has also evolved to enhance its worthiness, for example by changing its name from Mothers Against Drunk *Drivers* to Mothers Against Drunk *Driving* to reflect a focus on "the ways in which society, social policy, and government had contributed to the problem," rather than just focusing on "killer drunks."[18]

It is also possible to organize collective action around issues that might not resonate as personally as drunk driving. Private citizens in Canada, dismayed by the plight of the Vietnamese boat people after the United States pulled out of Vietnam, lobbied the Canadian government to allow for private sponsorship of these refugees, over and above the existing quotas for refugees and outside the normal parameters.[19] This resulted in the creation of the still-unique Private Sponsorship of Refugees Program in 1979, which has since facilitated the private sponsorship of 275,000 refugees. The private sponsors, typically faith-based communities or ethno-cultural groups, are able to name specific refugees in which they have interest and provide private financial support and settlement assistance for one year after arrival.[20] Except for extreme circumstances, a privately sponsored person will not be turned down by immigration authorities. The fact that the program is citizen driven and over and above the government-run immigration program helps shield it from political bickering, making the jobs of the politicians easier.

The program came to the fore again almost forty years later during the Syrian refugee crisis. Thanks to the care and work of Canadian citizens across the country, Canada was able to take a disproportionately high number of Syrian refugees, over fifty thousand, while avoiding much of the political furor that accompanied publicly run Syrian refugee immigration in the United States.[21] This represented a large and relatively successful application of collective action by citizens to get something done that governments likely could not or would not have done.

Collective action doesn't always work, of course. Moms Demand Action for Gun Sense in America, which was formed after the shooting disaster at Sandy Hook Elementary School in Newtown, Connecticut, and the march on Washington, led by students after the shooting at Marjory Stoneman Douglas High School in Parkland, Florida, were both backed by numbers (over 90 percent of Americans want comprehensive background checks for purchasers of firearms), commitment, unity, and worthiness, but neither has been able to spur the duopoly in Washington to take action on the issue.[22] The National Rifle Association, with its (self-reported) five million members, has managed to game politics in a sufficiently strategic way that has allowed an organization representing 1.5 percent of Americans to override the wishes of 90 percent of Americans. That case notwithstanding, in many instances, citizens can and do leverage collective action to create political frictions without which the political system, left to its own devices, would take the status quo as its efficient outcome.

Insist on Reciprocal Political Relationships

Relationships between citizens and their elected officials are increasingly becoming one-sided and passive. This imbalance in engagement enables political leaders to become ensconced in power, maintaining a status quo that is comfortable for them. This passivity works against citizens' interests.

It unfolds like this. Politicians identify a set of problems that attract widespread concern or even fear. Then they promise a solution that will require no action from voters other than electing those very same politicians. A textbook example of this approach was the 1994 midterm elections, when the Republicans gained fifty-six House seats and nine Senate seats to take control of both houses of Congress for the first time in fifty-two years.

Widely credited with this success was the Newt Gingrich–inspired "Contract with America," which promised eight major legislative reforms and ten specific bills that would be enacted if America voted in Republican congressional majorities.[23] While Gingrich's proposal was a "contract" in some very basic sense, it was pretty one-sided. The electorate was asked to do one simple thing on one single day—pull a lever for a Republican congressional candidate in a polling station—and the politicians would do absolutely everything else for them.

Of course, big promises had been made before. But the Contract with America represented a 180-degree shift from the spirit of John F. Kennedy's 1961 inaugural address, in which he admonished the electorate to "Ask not what your country can do for you—ask what you can do for your country." The Contract with America was such a strikingly successful formula that it deepened and solidified the trend by which politicians make disproportionate promises while encouraging citizens to feel that they have no responsibilities for doing anything. When politicians fail to produce what was promised, which is inevitable, voters complain bitterly but readily fall for an opposition that is selling an equally one-sided contract. In effect, a passive citizenry colludes with politicians to set up a series of failures, reinforcing disengagement from an apparently paralyzed democratic system. It is not hard to see where this is leading the United States and many other democracies.

Yet citizen engagement used to be a defining feature of the American system. At the beginning of the nineteenth century, the French political philosopher Alexis de Tocqueville famously undertook a journey around the early United States in an effort to understand the new experiment with democracy. The result—in effect, an exercise in what we would today call ethnographical research—was *Democracy in America*, which remains required reading for students of political science and history the world over. In that book, Tocqueville emphasizes the key importance of engagement by ordinary citizens in protecting the political system created by the Founding Fathers.[24]

That spirit survives in many ways—Americans remain keen to volunteer and will collectively engage on many issues, as we have seen, for instance, with MADD. But as American political scientist Robert Putnam has perceptively pointed out, thanks in large part to cheap and easy in-home entertainment, Americans increasingly "bowl alone," and this trend has further shaped their disengagement from social activities—including politics—in recent decades.[25] Their relationship with politicians has been reduced to a transaction: "You tell me what I want to hear, and I'll vote for you. If I don't think what you tell me you'll do works for me, I'll vote for the other guy." This dynamic hardly reflects the engagement with the political process that Tocqueville observed. So by implying that all voters needed to do with regard to making laws was to cast a vote (no further engagement necessary), Newt Gingrich's Contract with America, whatever its merits or demerits as a legislative agenda, represented a turning away from the spirit upon which American democracy was founded.

This is not enough to underpin American democratic capitalism. Citizens need not only to accept joint responsibility for making newer, better things happen, but to actually participate in making them happen. Only then can they push political leaders to balance efficiency with resilience by asking their electorate to contribute, instead of that electorate just sitting back and waiting for political leaders to take actions that they are not, in fact, going to take. Only when American citizens ask for and carry out a bigger role in the future of their country will there be positive adaptation in a system that has adapted away from delivering the benefits citizens expect.

What will that engagement involve? A good example of citizens sharing responsibility for producing success is a civic innovation known as participatory budgeting. In participatory budgeting, a government entity—and thus far it has been municipal governments—sets aside a pool of funding for participatory budgeting proposals. Residents of the community self-organize to brainstorm project ideas and create formal proposals for the strongest ideas. Then there is a formal voting process in which the residents vote on which projects they believe would benefit the community most. The government entity—i.e., the municipality—then funds as many of the projects as its budget allows, following the order of priority established by community votes.[26]

Participatory budgeting began in Porto Alegre, Brazil, in 1989 but has spread to more than three thousand cities around the world since then, including New York City, which tested out a participatory-budgeting program in 2012 and has spent $210 million on 706 different community projects since then. In 2018, just under one hundred thousand residents participated in the program to allocate $36 million for investments in schools, parks, and libraries.[27]

While small in the overall picture, participatory budgeting has shown the capacity for getting more citizens involved in the day-to-day processes of politics, especially citizens for whom participation has generally seemed futile. In the New York process, almost twice the proportion of families with household income under $35,000 took part in participatory budgeting as voted in municipal elections. The same was true for other important demographic groupings: Hispanics and those under the age of twenty-four were also twice as likely to vote in participatory-budgeting exercises as in elections.[28] Clearly, participatory budgeting encourages citizens to play a part more in day-to-day political decision making and helps them learn how to structure more-reciprocal relationships with their elected governments, thereby better positioning themselves to contribute to a more resilient economy. Kennedy and Tocqueville would certainly have approved—and I'd venture that Robert Putnam would as well.

Make Each Vote Count

We've already seen that many voters have reduced their engagement to the ballot box. Bad as it is for democracy for citizen engagement with politicians to be reduced to a biennial (for House members) or quadrennial (for presidents) or sexennial (for senators) vote, politicians have found ways to secure their own positions even more by reducing the power of that vote through a process that has come to be called gerrymandering. The name recognizes—not in a good way—Massachusetts Governor Elbridge Gerry, who signed a bill to approve a district with voting characteristics favorable to his party, a district shaped like a salamander.

The system of representative government was designed to have members of the House of Representatives represent districts that are geographically logical and whose membership is politically diverse. Members of the Senate represent an entire state and were originally chosen by the state legislature but are now chosen by a statewide vote.

While there was no mandate that candidates needed to be a member of a political party in the initial design of the congressional game, the system has adapted such that in congressional races there have been only two consequential parties since 1854. Only five House and eight Senate independents have been elected since World War II, and the pattern of each was or has been to vote and caucus with one of the two dominant parties.[29] The most recent genuine third-party candidate to win a House seat was a liberal in 1949. The most recent to win a Senate seat was a conservative in 1971. And neither of those represented a meaningful deviation from the two dominant parties. The most recent third-party presidential candidate to earn a single electoral college vote was George Wallace in 1968, with 46 of 538 electoral college votes.[30]

The bottom line is that the system whereby politicians are elected has adapted to entrench a duopoly that was last breached, and then only modestly and temporarily, half a century ago. There are extremely high barriers to the successful entry of a third party, as existing parties have powerful and typically well-funded national party structures. It is very handy for those parties to maintain the duopoly and for individual politicians to insulate themselves as much as possible from the power of citizens—who can theoretically vote them out of office every two, four, or six years.

Gerrymandering is a particularly powerful way of insulating politicians from being voted out. It involves manipulating the geographic shapes of districts in order to group together voters with either a distinctly Democratic or distinctly Republican voting bent so that the race is not really contested. It is a safe seat, for one or the other party. There can be no more vivid representation of the product of a complex adaptive system than the Third Congressional District of Maryland, called America's most gerrymandered district by *The New Republic* (see figure 9-1). In this case, the gerrymandering produces a safe Democratic seat. Similarly gerrymandered districts produce safe Republican seats.

This gerrymandering serves a very specific purpose: to make certain that no individual's vote in that district really matters. The election is a foregone conclusion. It is thanks to practices like this that 93 percent of incumbent House members who have sought reelection since 1964 have succeeded.[31] Their only competition comes from within their own party, and historically parties prefer incumbents, who are more familiar with the workings of the system, which in any event still favors seniority in allocating positions on important congressional committees. It is in part because an entire state can't be gerrymandered that successful Senate incumbency over the same period is somewhat lower—though it is still absolutely very high—at 83 percent.[32]

FIGURE 9–1

The Third Congressional District of Maryland

Source: 116th Congress of the United States, Maryland—Congressional District 3, United States Census Bureau, https://www2.census.gov/geo/maps/cong_dist/cd116/cd_based/ST24/CD116_MD03.pdf.

Gerrymandering is an inevitable result of the rational pursuit of self-interest in a game where the rules do not put sufficient constraints on the involvement of politicians in the drawing of constituency boundaries, and it has produced an outcome that is in the interests of the most powerful actors—the duopoly political parties. The votes of many citizens just don't count. And of course, the further adaptation to that phenomenon is that voters whose votes don't matter choose not to bother to vote, producing ever lower voter turnout; again, a very sensible adaptation on their part, given the game in which they are asked to play.

But citizens are not powerless against gerrymandering—even if political parties enthusiastically support it. For example, in 2000, an umbrella citizen's group in Arizona called Fair Districts, Fair Elections successfully sought to put a referendum on the 2000 election ballot that would curtail partisan gerrymandering by putting redistricting in the hands of a politically independent commission. The amendment won a 56.1 percent referendum majority, and Arizona has featured an independent redistricting commission ever since.[33]

A decade later a citizens campaign led by lawyer Ellen Freidin succeeded in putting together a coalition called Fair Districts Florida to collect the 1.7 million signatures necessary to put an anti-gerrymandering amendment on the November 2, 2010, Florida ballot. As with the Arizona vote, the measure won a substantial majority—62.6 percent—resulting in a circuit-court judge ordering the redrawing of two gerrymandered districts. When the Florida legislature attempted to subvert the judge's intentions, Fair Districts Florida appealed the redistricting to the state supreme court. The supreme court ruled in favor of the appeal and ordered the nonpartisan redrawing of not only the two contentious districts but another six as well—while issuing a scathing criticism of the legislature's behavior in the wake of the referendum.[34]

A Michigan group called Voters Not Politicians collected over 425,000 signatures to get a proposal on the November 2018 ballot to create an Independent Citizens Redistricting Commission, and it passed with a 61 percent majority. Citizen groups in Missouri, Ohio, Colorado, and Utah followed suit.[35] Although the Supreme Court voted in June 2019 not to tackle gerrymandering at the federal level, citizens can still take collective action at the state level to beat back gerrymandering and make more votes really count.

Given that the current adaptation favors the political party leadership and elected politicians, reinforced by moneyed interests, citizens cannot expect them to drive future adaptation in directions favorable to the average American citizen. This is where citizens need to step up to a tough task and make their voices heard to drive redistricting in a direction that causes a higher percentage of American votes to actually count. This is a goal entirely independent of political party. Every citizen has an incentive to make more votes count. Citizens need to apply pressure on candidates and sitting politicians to prioritize the cause of redistricting.

Gerrymandering is not the only factor contributing to the job security of politicians. The other key factor is simply that people don't sign up to vote. This used to be (and arguably still is) deliberately engineered—a notable example being the suppression of African American voter registration. But although the most egregious abuses of voter rights have largely been consigned to history, American voters are not encouraged to sign up and vote. The US voter registration rate of 74 percent of eligible voters compares poorly with neighboring Canada's 93 percent rate. Low participation rates in US elections compound the effect of this. For example, 2018 was the first midterm election since 1982 in which half or more of the US voting-age population actually cast ballots (53.4 percent). However, less than 40 percent of eligible voters under the age of twenty-nine did so.[36] Presidential election years draw slightly higher turnout, but it hasn't hit 60 percent since 1968. This low level of participation should be a long-term concern to all parties invested in democratic capitalism, given the consequences of voter disengagement. But considering that low participation suits the immediate interests of party machines, solutions will have to be forced onto the system by voters.

There are working solutions for which voters could press. In Canada, for example, it is the job of a federal agency to get as high a percentage of eligible voters registered as possible. Elections

Canada works with over forty other agencies to get up-to-date addresses in order to register voters and inform them which polling station they should report to for voting.[37] Fellow former British colony Australia is even more extreme where registration is concerned, and even closer to perfection—96 percent. On top of that, voting is compulsory.[38] And while Canada and Australia are not precisely like America, their democratic-capitalist systems are similar and have not been diminished in any observable way by automatic registration.

Automatic voter registration isn't even a foreign concept in America. Oregon introduced automatic voter registration to the country as of January 1, 2016, and since then, twelve states plus the District of Columbia have followed suit, including two of the country's largest states, California and Illinois.[39] There is evidence of success elsewhere, and momentum across US states. Citizens should continue to apply pressure to get registration to be automatic in all fifty states so that every potential voter has a chance to be counted. The effort of applying this pressure would, by itself, generate engagement in a pressing political issue, and its outcome would be to put more friction, in the form of citizen votes, into the excessively well-oiled political machines that still dominate American politics.

Getting Started

The failure of gun-control efforts illustrates why none of this will be easy. Recall that this book started with the striking political disengagement of the regular Americans we interviewed for the MPI Persona Project. Their wistfulness was palpable. Part of that was because they knew they should be more involved and less disengaged. But part was also the feeling of not knowing how they would get started.

My advice is to start very small with something very easy. Use your inherent purchasing power from your existing purchasing patterns. Next time you are on the verge of buying a product or service from your dominant provider, pick an alternative instead. You will have struck a tiny but important blow for friction and against Pareto distributions. For your subsequent purchase, you can return to the dominant provider—just don't do it 100 percent of the time.

Then think about taking collective action in your own area on something that is close to you. Don't try to change the world profoundly. Change something little and close to home. The Love Canal families tackled something local and personal. They wanted their back yards cleaned up. Their actions ended up driving the creation of the Environmental Protection Agency's Superfund, which changed America.

Next, go to political campaign events and ask candidates what they want you to do to contribute to a more successful American democratic capitalism. If they respond "donate to my campaign," ask them to try again. Keep on asking until you get an answer that makes sense to you. Then ask them about gerrymandering and voter registration. Be insistent. Make it clear that these are questions that are important to you. Make it clear you are not going to go away.

None of these things is terribly big or terribly complicated, but each will contribute positively to the future of democratic capitalism. And while citizens on their own cannot expect to bring about fundamental change—for that, we will also need the contributions of executives, politicians, and educators along the lines already discussed—the steps you as a citizen take are vital to pushing and cajoling executives, politicians, and educators to play the parts they need to play.

Chapter 10

Closing Thoughts

The future of American democratic capitalism is clouded. It is possible that we will be able to overcome our obsession with economic efficiency. And it is possible that we will not. For the former to happen, it will take a lot of work and commitment by many Americans. I will describe the contrasting scenarios first and then conclude this book with a call to action for American business executives, political leaders, educators, and citizens.

American Democratic Capitalism: A Tale of Two Futures

I am both pessimistic and optimistic about America's future. That combination of concern and hope has six elements. First, I worry about the current path while remaining confident that there is an alternative. Second, I doubt that any one group or person can set us on that other path, yet I believe that we will reach it thanks to the contributions of many. Third, I cannot see that there exists any one solution that will fix the system, yet I am sure that by applying many solutions in combination we can correct our course. Fourth, I fear that we will stumble if we go in with a grand strategy, yet I believe that by taking small steps we can go far. Fifth, I fear that we will fail in our endeavors if we hew to ideologies, yet I am confident that we will succeed if we remain reflective in our practice. Finally, I think we will fail if we sit and debate the way forward, yet I know that we can succeed if we start acting now.

Current path versus alternative path

On its current path, American democratic capitalism is, I believe, heading for an ugly fall. I do not believe that it can survive the Pareto outcomes that are becoming more evident. On its own, capitalism might be capable. China may continue to evolve in a way that demonstrates that capitalism without democracy can work. By most measures, inequality is higher in China than in the United States, but without democracy, that isn't a big vulnerability because China's citizens can't vote the Communist Party out of power. In America, though, citizens do have votes, and they can vote to end the country's magical combination of democracy and capitalism. That is why we need American democratic capitalism to produce outcomes that are sufficiently Gaussian, to provide a resilient base.

But that can't happen unless we collectively abandon the machine model of the economy along with the accompanying, obsessive pursuit of efficiency. If we do discard this now well-entrenched model, along with its obsession, and instead recognize that we live in a complex adaptive system that needs balance in the pursuits of efficiency and resilience, then I am optimistic that American democratic capitalism will have a bright future—a future that builds on all of democratic capitalism's great accomplishments over the past two hundred and fifty years.

One group versus multiple groups

No one person or group can bring about the necessary shift for a resilient future. No president can fix it himself or herself. No political party, not even the two dominant parties together, can. Nor can business executives or educators. In any complex adaptive system, numerous participants interact with each another to generate the observed outcomes. It would be foolish self-importance for any one person or group to think that he, she, or it alone could produce dramatically improved outcomes, and it would be delusional to ask one person or group to take sole responsibility for fixing the problem. That would be possible only if the system were not complex and adaptive. Then an individual or group could focus on the one big leverage point, fix it, and drive dramatic positive change. However, if one group attempts to fundamentally change a complex adaptive system, the rest of the system can easily overwhelm, counteract, and/or game the intervention.

But I am optimistic that if business executives, political leaders, educators, *and* citizens take positive steps, even if they don't intentionally coordinate with one another, the requisite change will commence. A positive future for American democratic capitalism needs contribution from everyone. That is both good and bad. On the one hand, it means we can't wait for one savior to take action. On the other hand, it means that everyone can contribute and be part of a positive solution—and needs to be.

One solution versus a combination of many

No single initiative can make a meaningful change in our current course, even if business executives, political leaders, educators, and citizens join into and support that single initiative. The performance of a complex adaptive system is not improved dramatically with the pulling of a single lever. That too is a delusion. Tax reform won't do it. Educational reform won't do it. Financial-market reforms won't do it. What's more, in a complex adaptive system, the unintended consequences of a singular big, bold move can often undo the hoped-for benefits of that one move and even make a bad situation worse. This has happened too many times for that outcome to be ignored or underestimated.

Instead we should pursue a wide variety of initiatives aimed at improving the functioning of democratic capitalism. This kind of tweaking will enable us to change the trajectory of the system without falling prey to debilitating unintended consequences. That is why I have laid out eighteen initiatives across four groups of actors. We don't have to do every single one of them to make a meaningful difference. But it will probably require progress on a majority of them to drive the transformation that we need.

Starting big versus starting small

We will be in trouble if we convince ourselves that we have to start big—arguing to ourselves that it is a big problem and only big solutions will get the job done. Once again, that is delusional in a complex adaptive system. Complex adaptive systems don't generally take well to big step-function changes—a bit like the dinosaurs attempting to react to dramatic climate change. If we knew for sure that a big step-function change was actually in the right direction, it might work. But with a complex adaptive system, not even the smartest mind can know with reasonable certainty—if any certainty at all—what the best direction is. In this context, big is definitely not better.

So, we should start small, ending up with dramatic change at the end of many small steps. That was my approach at the Rotman School. My goal from the beginning was to have a Rotman

School in my last year as dean that was unrecognizable as a descendent of the Rotman School I had inherited in my first year as dean. However, I wanted the change in each year to be so small that it wouldn't cause anyone—students, professors, staff, alumni, university administrators, recruiters—to be worried or upset enough to fight the change. It worked: without overly worrying anybody along the way, we transformed the Rotman School utterly in fifteen years. When outsiders looked retrospectively at the change, they viewed it as transformational. Insiders, in contrast, saw it as evolutionary or even incremental. While it would be nice to be able to say every step along the way was according to plan, it would be patently false. The intent stayed the same, but the plan to get there was tweaked and tweaked and tweaked as the consequences of previous tweaks became apparent.

Ideological versus reflective

We cannot be ideological about the changes that need to be made. To be ideological is to believe that our model is correct as it stands today and should guide all of our actions. Even worse, a core element of many ideologies is the belief that if someone does not share the ideology in question, then he or she is in some way malevolent—e.g., undependable, dangerous, malicious, or nefarious. As I have pointed out repeatedly, all models are wrong. They are all interpretations of the world that enable us to take action; shortcuts, as it were. When we are ideological, we are closed to the process of learning and improvement. Ideologues don't tweak.

Let us instead have a strong point of view, weakly held. That stance will cause us to be open to feedback from the complex adaptive system that we are attempting to improve. Rather than defend flawed models and initiatives because we are unreflectively attached to them, we should be reflective about our models, the better to tweak our models and initiatives quickly and repeatedly. If we are reflective about our models, we will never cease tweaking them for the better.

Debate versus action

We cannot afford to argue about whether there is a problem to solve in the first place and if so, what the single optimal approach to it is. Unfortunately, that is standard operating procedure in the modern economy. When a model doesn't produce the desired results, the dominant reaction is to argue that it hasn't been given enough time to work. And if that argument don't compel, the next most common argument is that the model has not been applied with enough intensity. As a consequence, we feel compelled to double down on existing models and argue about the results before we can even start the process of building a better model.

We should just get started and make course corrections as we go. Neither the status quo nor any one idea for changing it is precious. Forward progress for American democratic capitalism is the only precious thing; the only thing we should care about.

Where from Here?

While American democratic capitalism has always been far from perfect, no complex adaptive system the world has ever seen has been perfect. Nor will it or any complex adaptive system be in the future. America has made many mistakes in its application of democratic capitalism, whether through the actions of business executives, political leaders, educators, or citizens—or combinations thereof. However, America has also shown the world the promise of democratic capitalism to provide progress for the many.

Closing Thoughts

My optimism overwhelms my pessimism. The core reason is that there are no obstacles to acting on the agenda I have laid out other than entirely self-imposed ones. We don't need permission to pursue an alternative path. We don't have to ask whether it is OK to involve multiple groups. There is nothing stopping us from pursuing multiple initiatives or from starting with small initiatives and building from there. We can all choose to be reflective about our models. And absolutely nothing is standing between us and getting started.

Really, there is no excuse to not just get started. The downside of the status quo is staring Americans in the collective face. Our obsession with economic efficiency has featured too much pressure, too much connectedness, and too much pursuit of perfection, all of which has produced a dangerously unbalanced economy lacking resilience. But collectively, we can restore balance if we just get started, stay reflective, and tweak relentlessly. And because the outcomes in a complex adaptive system aren't linear, incremental, and predictable, we will have no idea just how good a future American democratic capitalism could have. America's next chapter could be the greatest in its history!

Notes

Introduction

1. The conversations in this chapter are taken from personal interviews with the subjects. The names have been changed for privacy.

2. US Census Bureau, "Historical Income Tables: Families," https://www.census.gov/data/tables/time-series/demo/income-poverty/historical-income-families.html.

3. Author's calculations based on US Census Bureau data. Thanks to the work of Thomas Picketty and Emmanuel Saez, who created the World Inequality Database (WID; https://wid.world/world/), we now have estimates of various incomes from earlier periods. I have used the US Census Bureau data because it is the official US government data. However, it is useful to compare the results to those provided by the WID. The match is not perfect because income is calculated somewhat differently. But the advantage is the ability to go back to 1929, the peak income year before the onset of the Great Depression. If the census data for the period 1947–1976 is replaced with the WID data for 1929–1976, and 1976–2018 census with 1976–2014 WID (the last year of its time series), the WID shows an even greater drop in median income growth in the two periods: the census shows a drop from 2.4 percent to 0.6 percent; the WID, a drop from 3.3 percent to 0.6 percent.

4. Author's calculations based on US Census Bureau data. Again, the WID data is confirmatory and makes the argument stronger. It shows income of the average of the fiftieth and fifty-first percentile for adults (an approximation of the median) returned to the 1929 peak in eight years rather than ten, and doubled in fourteen years rather than fifteen.

5. Author's calculations based on US Bureau of Economic Analysis data.

6. Raj Chetty et al., "The Fading American Dream: Trends in Absolute Income Mobility Since 1940," working paper 22910, The National Bureau of Economic Research, Cambridge, 2016, revised 2017.

7. Richard V. Burkhauser, Jeff Larrimore, and Kosali I. Simon, "A 'Second Opinion' on the Economic Health of the American Middle Class," working paper 17164, The National Bureau of Economic Research, Cambridge, 2011.

8. Gerald Auten and David Splinter, "Income Inequality in the United States: Using Tax Data to Measure Long-Term Trends," Staff of the Joint Committee on Taxation, December 20, 2019.

9. Michael E. Porter, *The Competitive Advantage of Nations* (New York: Simon & Schuster, 1989).

Notes

Chapter 1

1. Svetlana A. Kaliadina and Natal'ia Iu. Pavlova, "The Family of W. W. Leontief in Russia," *Economic Systems Research* 18, no. 4 (2006): 335.

2. "Wassily Leontief Biographical," The Nobel Prize (website), https://www.nobelprize.org/prizes/economic-sciences/1973/leontief/biographical/; "Wassily Leontief Biography," The Famous People (website), https://www.thefamouspeople.com/profiles/wassily-leontief-299.php.

3. See, for example, Wassily Leontief, "An Alternative to Aggregation in Input-Output Analysis and National Accounts," *The Review of Economics and Statistics* 49, no. 3 (1967): 412.

4. Soma Golden, "The Economy: Next 25 Years," *The New York Times*, December 29, 1974.

5. In my entire time there, I didn't come across another student from a town of under 100 in population, though there may well have been others. However, I was later encouraged to find out that superstar economist John Kenneth Galbraith, who was then in the twilight of his luminous career in the Harvard economics department, was born and raised in Iona Station, a farm-country hamlet less than 100 miles away from and as small as my own home of Wallenstein, in Southern Ontario.

6. From a veritable Who's Who of famous economists, including Galbraith, Otto Eckstein, Martin Feldstein, John Dunlop, James Duesenberry, and Arthur Smithies, not to mention as yet unrecognized luminaries such as Michael Spence, who would go on to win his Nobel in 2001.

7. John D. Sterman, "All Models Are Wrong: Reflections on Becoming a Systems Scientist," *Systems Dynamics Review* 18, no. 4 (2002): 501.

8. George E. P. Box, "Science and Statistics," *Journal of the American Statistical Association* 71, no. 356 (1976): 791.

9. John D. Sterman, from a lecture at the Rotman School of Management, University of Toronto, 2006.

10. Winston Churchill, on rebuilding the Chamber of Commons following its destruction during the Blitz (HC Deb 28 October 1943, vol. 393, cc. 403–73), https://api.parliament.uk/historic-hansard/commons/1943/oct/28/house-of-commons-rebuilding.

11. Frederick F. Reichheld, *The Loyalty Effect: The Hidden Force behind Growth, Profits, and Lasting Value* (Boston: Harvard Business School Press, 1996).

12. Frederick F. Reichheld, "The One Number You Need to Grow," *Harvard Business Review*, December 2003.

13. Ray Dalio, "How the Economic Machine Works," September 22, 2013, Video, 31:00, https://youtu.be/PHe0bXAIuk0.

14. Peter Drucker, from a lecture at the Rotman School of Management, University of Toronto, 2001.

15. Author's calculations based on National Center for Education Statistics data.

16. The model has its roots in Gauss's research into astronomical observation errors.

17. The biggest country with income higher than the United States is the oil-rich United Arab Emirates, with a population of 9.5 million, about 3 percent the size of the United States, equivalent to the country's eleventh-biggest state.

18. David Lundberg and Henry F. May, "The Enlightened Reader in America," *American Quarterly* 28, no. 2 (1976): 262.

19. Alexander Hamilton, *Report on the Subject of Manufactures,* submitted to the House of Representatives, December 5, 1791.

20. David Ricardo, *On the Principles of Political Economy and Taxation* (London: John Murray, 1817).

21. The US became the world's largest gross exporter in 1898 and maintained that position nearly uninterrupted for one hundred years. Author's calculations from CEPII data, available at http://www.cepii.fr/CEPII/en/bdd_modele/presentation.asp?id=32.

22. Chad P. Bown and Douglas A. Irwin, "The GATT's Starting Point: Tariff Levels Circa 1947," working paper 21782, The National Bureau of Economic Research, Cambridge, 2015.

23. Frederick Winslow Taylor, *The Principles of Scientific Management* (New York: Harper & Brothers, 1911), 64.

Chapter 2

1. John Perry and Heather Vogell "Are Drastic Swings in CRCT Scores Valid?" *The Atlanta Journal-Constitution*, October 19, 2009.

2. WXIA-TV, Atlanta, "11 Atlanta Educators Convicted in Cheating Scandal," April 1, 2015, and Rhonda Cook, "New Mother Gets Prison, Former Principal Jail in APS Case," *The Atlanta Journal-Constitution*, September 1, 2015.

3. Michael Harris and Bill Tayler, "Don't Let Metrics Undermine Your Business," *Harvard Business Review*, September–October 2019.

4. Jackie Wattles, Ben Geier, and Matt Egan, "Wells Fargo's 17-Month Nightmare," CNNMoney, February 5, 2018.

5. Roger L. Martin, "The Rise (and Likely Fall) of the Talent Economy," *Harvard Business Review,* October 2014.

6. "Billionaires: The Richest People in the World," *Forbes*, March 5, 2019.

7. John Doerr, *Measure What Matters: How Google, Bono, and the Gates Foundation Rock the World with OKRs* (New York: Portfolio, 2018).

8. William J. Kolasky and Andrew R. Dick, "The Merger Guidelines and the Integration of Efficiencies into Antitrust Review of Horizontal Mergers," *Antitrust Law Journal* 71, no. 1 (2003): 207.

9. Alberto Wallis, "The Wireless Carrier Market: A Two-Horse Race," *Seeking Alpha*, June 24, 2019. https://seekingalpha.com/article/4271824-wireless-carrier-market-two-horse-race.

10. Matthew Chiasson and Paul A. Johnson, "Canada's (In)efficiency Defence: Why Section 96 May Do More Harm Than Good for Economic Efficiency and Innovation," *Canadian Competition Law Review* 32, no. 1 (2019): 1.

11. Kolasky and Dick, "The Merger Guidelines."

Notes

12. Matthew Stewart, *The Management Myth: Debunking Modern Business Philosophy* (New York: W. W. Norton, 2009).

Chapter 3

1. Vilfredo Pareto, "The Curve of the Distribution of Wealth," translated by John Caincross for *History of Economic Ideas,* vol. 17, no. 1 (2009): 132–143. Pareto's paper was originally published in 1896.

2. John Przybys, "At 7-Foot-8, Las Vegas Man is Comfortable in His Frame," *Las Vegas Review Journal,* October 3, 2019, https://www.reviewjournal.com/life/at-7-foot-8-las-vegas-man-is-comfortable-in-his-frame-1863169/.

3. Statistics for number of followers from Instagram.com, accessed May 2020.

4. For an original discussion on what became known as preferential attachment, see Derek J. de Solla Price, "Networks of Scientific Papers," *Science* 149, no. 3683 (1965): 510.

5. Pierpaolo Andriani and Bill McKelvey, "Using Scale-Free Processes to Explain Punctuated-Change in Management-Relevant Phenomena," *International Journal of Complexity in Leadership and Management* 1, no. 3 (2011): 211.

6. Net worth statistics from therichest.com, accessed June 2019.

7. Fabian Gorsler, "Here's How Much 10 of the World's Biggest Celebrities Make on Instagram Per Post," *Business Insider,* July 26, 2018.

8. The North American Free Trade Agreement (NAFTA) came into force on January 1, 1994. It superseded the Canada–United States Free Trade Agreement of 1988.

9. Observers like to combine the effects of globalization and technology by pointing out that the rich are made up of individuals who built a global technology company. Indeed, there is more than a grain of truth in this argument. A great way to get rich in modern America is to found (or build) a global technology company. There are 75 such people on the 2019 *Forbes* 400 list of the richest Americans. However, almost as good a way to become superrich is to manage other people's money and get paid 2% of assets under management plus 20% of the upside (the famous 2&20 formula) by running either a hedge, LBO, or venture fund. That accounts for 63 members of the same list. This is an industry centered dominantly in America, one that makes the majority of its returns buying and selling on US stock exchanges. In addition, another 147 members of that 400-person list (37%) run decidedly national-scope companies in not-yet-globalized industries such as real estate, health care, and telecommunications services. In total, over half of the individuals on the *Forbes* 400 either made their fortune running an investment fund or a domestic company, rather than an obviously global enterprise or one based on technology. (Author's calculations based on the 2019 *Forbes* 400.)

10. Christopher Ingraham. "The Richest 1 Percent Now Owns More of the Country's Wealth Than at Any Time in the Past 50 Years," *The Washington Post,* December 6, 2017.

11. Michael E. Porter, *The Competitive Advantage of Nations* (New York: Simon & Schuster, 1989).

Notes

12. Richard Florida, *The Rise of the Creative Class* (New York: Basic Books, 2002).

13. Kathleen M. Kahle and René M. Stulz, "Is the US Public Corporation in Trouble?" *Journal of Economic Perspectives* 31, no. 3 (2017): 67.

14. The Almond Board of California, "California Almond Industry Facts," June 2016, http://www.almonds.com/sites/default/files/2016_almond_industry_factsheet.pdf.

15. See, for example, Byard Duncan, "California's Almond Harvest Has Created a Golden Opportunity for Bee Thieves," *Reveal*, October 8, 2018.

16. Jim Donnelly, "The Irish Famine," *BBC History*, February 17, 2011.

Chapter 4

1. Aspen Publishers, Blue Chip Economic Indicators, December 10, 2008.

2. Kimberly Amadeo, "2008 GDP, Growth, and Updates by Quarter," *The Balance*, June 25, 2019.

3. Congressional Budget Office, "Economic Effects of Reducing the Fiscal Restraint That Is Scheduled to Occur in 2013," May 2012.

4. Tim Harford, "An Astonishing Record—of Complete Failure," *Financial Times*, May 30, 2014.

5. John Berman, "Killer Whale: Ocean's Best Hunter Learns to Kill on Land," ABC News, February 4, 2010.

6. On one level, therefore, the Atlanta schoolteachers who surrogated test scores for educational outcomes were behaving entirely rationally as self-interested players. Doctoring the scores was a far easier, not to mention more lucrative, way to deliver better test results than teaching students better.

7. Michael C. Jensen, "Corporate Budgeting Is Broken—Let's Fix It," *Harvard Business Review*, November 2001, page 94.

8. Report of Anton R. Valukas, Examiner, "In re: Lehman Brothers Holdings Inc., *et al.*, Debtors. Chapter 11 Case No. 08-13555 (JMP) (Jointly Administered)," United States Bankruptcy Court, Southern District of New York, March 11, 2010. See in particular Volume 3 of 9, "Section III.A.4: Repo 105."

9. John Carney, "Report: Lehman Brothers Used 'Accounting Gimmick' to Hide the Size of Its Balance Sheet," *Business Insider*, March 11, 2010.

10. As it turned out, Lehman got its comeuppance, as the regulators decided to let the bank go bust once the other players in the repo markets cottoned on to the risks that Lehman had racked up and stopped accepting Lehman as a repo counterparty, thereby triggering a liquidity crisis. The regulators, who deemed Lehman small enough to fail, may have made the wrong decision, given the high connectivity between counterparties in the repo markets and the fact that Lehman was by no means the only financial institution heavily exposed to real-estate risk.

11. Eli Bartov, Dan Givoly, and Carla Hayn, "The Rewards to Meeting or Beating Earnings Expectations," *Journal of Accounting and Economics* 33, no. 2 (2002): 173.

12. Roger L. Martin, *Fixing the Game* (Boston: Harvard Business School Publishing, 2011).

13. Michael C. Jensen, "The Agency Costs of Overvalued Equity and the Current State of Corporate Finance," *European Financial Management* 10, no. 4 (2004): 549–565.

14. Jerry Adler, "Raging Bulls: How Wall Street Got Addicted to Light-Speed Trading," *Wired*, August 3, 2012.

15. Gregory Meyer, Nicole Bullock, and Joe Rennison, "How High-Frequency Trading Hit a Speed Bump," *Financial Times*, January 1, 2018.

16. David Schneider, "Financial Trading at the Speed of Light," *IEEE Spectrum*, September 23, 2011.

17. Author's calculations based on the 2019 *Forbes* 400.

18. Kathleen Kahle and René M. Stulz, "The Shrinking Number of Public Corporations in the US," LSE US Centre, http://bit.ly/2yWc6El.

19. See "Lobbying Data Summary," OpenSecrets.org Center for Responsive Politics, https://www.opensecrets.org/lobby/.

20. See "Stocks Traded, Total Value (Current US$)—United States," The World Bank, https://data.worldbank.org/indicator/CM.MKT.TRAD.CD ?locations=US.

21. See "Total Market Cap," NYSE, https://www.nyse.com/market-cap.

Chapter 5

1. Debt is cheaper than equity. To begin with, because interest payments on debt are deductible for corporate income-tax purposes and therefore companies get a subsidy from the Internal Revenue Service for using debt. Better yet, debt is considered less risky because debt holders are paid before any returns are paid to equity holders. Hence the required return that needs to be paid for debt is lower than for equity.

2. Tom Hals and Tracy Rucinski, "Toys 'R' Us Seeks Bankruptcy to Survive Retail Upheaval," Reuters, September 19, 2017; Todd Spangler, "iHeartMedia Bankruptcy Plan Approved, CEO Bob Pittman's Contract Renewed," *Variety*, January 22, 2019.

3. Tim Hornyak, "Clearing the Radioactive Rubble Heap That Was Fukushima Daiichi, 7 Years On," *Scientific American*, March 9, 2018.

4. Perry Arnold, "Why Can't Pitchers Throw as Many Innings as They Used To?" *Bleacher Report*, March 24, 2009.

5. In 2019, restrictor plates were being changed to tapered spacers, which are simply a more precise car part that produces the same effect as the plate. See, for example, "NASCAR Moving Away from Restrictor Plates, Not Pack Racing," Associated Press, February 15, 2019.

6. This section on design for adaptivity owes much to the work of Austrian philosopher of science Karl Popper, American pragmatist philosopher Charles Sanders Peirce, and Hungarian mathematician/philosopher Imre Lakatos, in particular to Lakatos's concept of "sophisticated methodological falsificationism." For helpful background, see Stephen Thornton, "Karl Popper," *The Stanford Encyclopedia of Philosophy*, Winter 2019 Edition; Robert Burch, "Charles Sanders Peirce," *The Stanford Encyclopedia of Philosophy*, Winter 2018 Edition;

and Imre Lakatos, *The Methodology of Scientific Research Programmes*, vol. 1 (Cambridge: Cambridge University Press, 1978).

7. See the discussion of the dangers of tightly coupled systems in Chris Clearfield and András Tilcsik, *Meltdown: Why Our Systems Fail and What We Can Do about It* (London: Penguin, 2018).

8. US–Canada Power System Outage Task Force, *Final Report on the August 14, 2003 Blackout in the United States and Canada: Causes and Recommendations*, April 2004.

9. See, for example, Joseph E. Stiglitz, "Capitalist Fools," *Vanity Fair*, January 2009.

10. Christine Romans, "Remembering the Worst Day in Wall Street History," CNNMoney, October 19, 2017.

11. John D. Sterman, "All Models Are Wrong: Reflections on Becoming a Systems Scientist," *Systems Dynamics Review* 18, no. 4 (2002): 501.

12. U.S. Securities and Exchange Commission, "Summary of 'Lessons Learned' from Events of September 11 and Implications for Business Continuity," February 13, 2002, https://www.sec.gov/divisions/marketreg/lessonslearned.htm.

13. Roger L. Martin, "Two Leading Researchers Discuss the Value of Oddball Data," *Harvard Business Review,* November 2009, 26–27.

14. FINRA, "2711. Research Analysts and Research Reports," FINRA Rules and Guidance, https://www.finra.org/rules-guidance/rulebooks/retired-rules/2711. Note that FINRA 2711 has been superseded by FINRA 2241, but the requirements for analyst disclosure on rating classification proportions remains intact.

Chapter 6

1. "Top 100," *Restaurant Business*, 2019, https://www.restaurantbusiness online.com/top-100-independents-2019?year=2019#data-table.

2. National Restaurant Association, "Hospitality Industry Turnover Rate Ticked Higher in 2018," May 9, 2019, https://restaurant.org/Articles/News/Hospitality-industry-turnover-rate-ticked-higher.

3. Roger L. Martin, personal interview with Stephen Sawitz and Jo Ann Bass at Joe's Stone Crab, Miami Beach, Florida, May 14, 2019.

4. Terri Williams, "America's Top CEOs and Their College Degrees," *Investopedia*, updated January 31, 2020, https://www.investopedia.com/articles/professionals/102015/americas-top-ceos-and-their-college-degrees.asp.

5. Shawn Tully, "The Big Number That Explains Kraft Heinz's Big Collapse," *Fortune*, February 28, 2019.

6. Zeynep Ton, *The Good Jobs Strategy* (New York: Houghton Mifflin Harcourt, 2014).

7. See, for example, Southwest's "Investor Relations" page, http://www.southwestairlinesinvestorrelations.com/our-company/proven-business-strategy.

8. Robert S. Kaplan and David P. Norton, "The Balanced Scorecard—Measures That Drive Performance," *Harvard Business Review,* January–February 1992.

Notes

9. Serkan Toto, "$1.45 Billion Record Fine: EU Slaps Intel Hard in Antitrust Case," *TechCrunch*, May 13, 2009.

10. Kurt Wagner, "'Stories' Was Instagram's Smartest Move Yet," *Vox*, August 8, 2018.

11. Ken Belson, "SBC Agrees to Acquire AT&T for $16 Billion," *The New York Times*, January 31, 2005.

12. Author's calculations based on S&P data.

Chapter 7

1. Paul Kosakowski, "The Fall of the Market in the Fall of 2008," *Investopedia*, June 25, 2019.

2. See CNNMoney, "Bailed Out Banks," https://money.cnn.com/news/specials/storysupplement/bankbailout/.

3. Francis Garrido and Saqib Chaudhry, "The World's 100 Largest Banks," S&P Global, April 5, 2019.

4. Neville Arjani and Graydon Paulin, "Lessons from the Financial Crisis: Bank Performance and Regulatory Reform," Bank of Canada Discussion Paper 2013–4, December 2013.

5. Julie Dickson, "Too Focused on the Rules: The Importance of Supervisory Oversight in Financial Regulation," *Cardozo Journal of International and Comparative Law* 18, no. 3 (2010): 623.

6. Rebecca Bream, "Canadian Bank Mergers: A Break with Tradition," Euromoney, April 30, 1998, https://www.euromoney.com/article/b1320dtygkvjg5/canadian-bank-mergers-a-break-with-tradition.

7. Robert J. Samuelson, "Why TARP Has Been a Success Story," *The Washington Post*, March 27, 2011.

8. Chris Isidore, "U.S. Ends TARP with $15.3 Billion Profit," CNNMoney, December 19, 2014.

9. Roger L. Martin, interview with the CEO of a public hospital in Ontario, Toronto, 2007.

10. Roger L. Martin, interview via telephone with Michael Bracken and Tom Loosemore, February 20, 2020.

11. See, for example, Dani Rodrik, "Populism and the Economics of Globalization," *Journal of International Business Policy* 1, nos. 1–2 (2018): 12.

12. Sean McLain, "Japan's Surging Car Exports Raise Risk of Trade Fight with Trump," *The Wall Street Journal*, April 19, 2018.

13. "Share of Foreign Car Sales in Japan Hit Record 9.1% in Fiscal 2017," *The Japan Times*, April 5, 2018; Jung Min-hee, "Market Share of Foreign Brand Cars Reaches New High in Korea," *Business Korea*, January 7, 2019.

14. Mark Scott, "Europe's Record Offers Cautions for a U.S. Battle with Google," *Politico*, June 2, 2019.

15. James Vincent, "Google Hit with €1.5 Billion Antitrust Fine by EU," *The Verge*, March 20, 2019.

16. John R. Graham, Campbell R. Harvey, and Shiva Rajgopal, "The Economic Implications of Corporate Financial Reporting," *Journal of Accounting and Economics* 40, nos. 1–3 (2005): 3.

17. Yvan Allaire, "Hedge Fund Activism: Preliminary Results and Some New Empirical Evidence," Institute for Governance of Private and Public Organizations, April 1, 2015.

18. Dan Marcec, "CEO Tenure Drops to Just Five Years," Equilar, January 19, 2018.

19. Full disclosure: I am an investor in the LTSE.

20. See, for example, Michael Lewis, *Flash Boys* (New York: W.W. Norton & Company, 2014).

21. Cezary Podkul, "Study Finds 'Speed Bumps' Help Protect Ordinary Investors," *The Wall Street Journal*, June 14, 2018.

22. Michael Stothard, "French Companies Fight Back against Florange Double-Vote Law," *Financial Times*, April 16, 2015.

23. "Historical Highest Marginal Income Tax Rates," Tax Policy Center, accessed January 18, 2019.

24. "H.R.4242—Economic Recovery Tax Act of 1981," https://www.congress.gov/bill/97th-congress/house-bill/4242.

25. "H.R.3838—Tax Reform Act of 1986," https://www.congress.gov/bill/99th-congress/house-bill/3838.

26. Roger L. Martin, "The Rise (and Likely Fall) of the Talent Economy," *Harvard Business Review*, October 2014, pages 40–47.

27. Author's calculations based on Tax Policy Center data.

28. Author's calculations based on 2019 estimates from the United States Census Bureau, and on Tanza Loudenback, "State Income Tax Rates across America, Ranked from Highest to Lowest," *Business Insider*, October 30, 2019.

Chapter 8

1. Josie Fung, I-Think Executive Director, and Nogah Kornberg, I-Think Associate Director, interview via telephone with Beth Grosso, Hamilton, Ontario, January 8, 2020.

2. Sabrina Stierwalt, "Is Pluto a Planet?" *Scientific American*, July 31, 2019.

3. For more information, see https://www.rotmanithink.ca/.

4. National Center for Education Statistics, "Graduate Degree Fields," updated April 2019.

5. Philip D. Arben, "The Integrating Course in the Business School Curriculum, or, Whatever Happened to Business Policy?" *Business Horizons* 40, no. 2 (1997): 65.

6. For more information, see http://www.rotman.utoronto.ca/FacultyAndResearch/ResearchCentres/DesautelsCentre/Integrative-Thinking.

7. Zach Church, "Professor Emeritus Jay Forrester, Digital Computing and System Dynamics Pioneer, Dies at 98." *MIT News*, November 19, 2016.

8. John German, "Conception to Birth: A Gleam in One Scientist's Eye," Santa Fe Institute, https://www.santafe.edu/about/history, accessed July 2019.

9. For more information, see https://necsi.edu.

10. Chris Argyris, *Overcoming Organizational Defenses: Facilitating Organizational Learning* (Boston: Allyn & Bacon, 1990).

Notes

11. Bruce Nussbaum, "The Power of Design," *BusinessWeek*, May 17, 2004.

12. Anne Strehlow, "Institute Launched to Bring 'Design Thinking' to Product Creation," Stanford News Service, October 11, 2005.

13. "Design Thinking: People First," *Economist*, January 10, 2018. https://www.economist.com/whichmba/design-thinking-people-first.

14. Stephen Gossett, "20 Design Thinking Courses You Should Know," *Built In*, November 25, 2019, https://builtin.com/design-ux/design-thinking-courses.

15. The twelve schools are Berkeley (Goldman), Chicago (Harris), Georgia (SPIA), Harvard (Kennedy), Indiana (O'Neill), Michigan (Ford), Minnesota (Humphrey), NYU (Wagner), Princeton (Woodrow Wilson), Southern California (Price), Syracuse (Maxwell), Washington (Evans).

16. I learned about this distinction from collaborator Hilary Austen, who attributes her understanding to her PhD supervisors, Jim March and Elliot Eisner, the late Stanford business and education professors, respectively.

17. National Center for Educational Statistics, "Digest of Educational Statistics, Table 318.30, Bachelor's, Master's, and Doctor's Degrees Conferred by Postsecondary Institutions, by Sex of Student and Discipline Division: 2017–18," https://nces.ed.gov/programs/digest/d19/tables/dt19_318.30.asp?current=yes.

18. Robin R. Wang, *Yinyang: The Way of Heaven and Earth in Chinese Thought and Culture* (Cambridge, UK: Cambridge University Press, 2012).

19. Aristotle, *Nicomachean Ethics*, trans. Robert C. Bartlett and Susan D. Collins (Chicago: University of Chicago Press, 2011).

20. See "MArts Anthropology with Innovation (XD50)," University of Bristol, https://www.bristol.ac.uk/study/undergraduate/2020/innovation/marts-anthropology-with-innovation/.

21. "Humanities and Science," Massachusetts Institute of Technology, http://catalog.mit.edu/interdisciplinary/undergraduate-programs/degrees/humanities-science/.

Chapter 9

1. Canadian ketchup story details from Claire Brownell, "The Condiment Wars: How a Misstep by Heinz Laid the Path for French's Quest to Become Canada's Ketchup King," *The Financial Post*, March 17, 2016, and Sophia Harris, "How French's Ketchup Took a Bite out of Heinz," *CBC News*, April 20, 2019.

2. "Loblaws Drops French's Ketchup from Its Shelves," *CBC News*, March 14, 2016.

3. Dalson Chen, "Loblaws to Re-Stock French's Ketchup after Public Outcry," *Windsor Star*, March 16, 2016.

4. "Loblaws Reverses Decision, Will Continue to Sell French's Ketchup," *CBC News*, March 15, 2016.

5. "Jo Ann Robinson: A Heroine of the Montgomery Bus Boycott," National Museum of African American History & Culture, https://nmaahc.si.edu/blog-post/jo-ann-robinson-heroine-montgomery-bus-boycott, accessed July 2019.

Notes

6. See www.buycott.com, accessed April 2019.

7. Ray Fisman and Tim Sullivan, "Don't Let Uber and Amazon Take Over the World," *USA Today*, December 16, 2016, https://www.usatoday.com/story/tech/columnist/2016/12/26/how--save--world-uber-and-amazon/95757208/.

8. Charles Tilly, "Social Movements as Historically Specific Clusters of Political Performances," *Berkeley Journal of Sociology* 38 (1993–1994): 1.

9. Brian Clark Howard, "SeaWorld to End Controversial Orca Shows and Breeding," *National Geographic*, March 17, 2016; Nestlé press release, "Nestlé Verifies Three-Quarters of Its Supply Chain as Deforestation-Free," April 30, 2019.

10. James C. Fell and Robert Voas, "Mothers Against Drunk Driving (MADD): The First 25 Years," *Traffic Injury Prevention* 7, no. 3 (2006): 195.

11. Ibid.

12. Ibid.

13. Frank J. Weed, "The MADD Queen: Charisma and the Founder of Mothers Against Drunk Driving," *The Leadership Quarterly* 4, nos. 3–4 (1993): 329.

14. Ibid.

15. Craig Reinarman, "The Social Construction of an Alcohol Problem: The Case of Mothers Against Drunk Drivers and Social Control in the 1980s," *Theory and Society* 17, no. 1 (1988): 91.

16. John D. McCarthy and Mark Wolfson, "Resource Mobilization by Local Social Movement Organizations: Agency, Strategy, and Organization in the Movement against Drinking and Driving," *American Sociological Review* 61, no. 6 (1996): 1070.

17. Mark Wolfson, "The Legislative Impact of Social Movement Organizations: The Anti-Drunken-Driving Movement and the 21-Year-Old Drinking Age," *Social Science Quarterly* 76, no. 2 (1995): 311.

18. Barry M. Sweedler, "The Role of Mothers Against Drunk Driving (MADD) in Reducing Alcohol-Related Crashes in the U.S.," *Traffic Injury Prevention* 7, no. 3 (2006): 193.

19. See, for example, The Canadian Encyclopedia, "Canadian Response to the 'Boat People' Refugee Crisis," https://www.thecanadianencyclopedia.ca/en/article/canadian-response-to-boat-people-refugee-crisis, accessed July 2019.

20. See, for example, the Canadian Council for Refugees, https://ccrweb.ca/en.

21. Peter Shawn Taylor, "How Syrian Refugees to Canada Have Fared Since 2015," *Maclean's*, May 21, 2019.

22. Quinnipiac Poll, "U.S. Voter Support for Abortion Is High, Quinnipiac University National Poll Finds; 94 Percent Back Universal Gun Background Checks," May 22, 2019.

23. Peter Feuerherd, "The Midterms That Changed America," *JSTOR Daily* (online newsletter), September 17, 2018, https://daily.jstor.org/the-midterms-that-changed-america/.

24. Alexis de Tocqueville, *Democracy in America* (London: Saunders and Otley, 1835, 1840).

Notes

25. Robert D. Putnam, *Bowling Alone: The Collapse and Revival of American Community* (New York: Simon & Schuster, 2000).

26. See, for example, the Participatory Budgeting Project, https://www .participatorybudgeting.org.

27. Josh Lerner, "Participatory Budgeting in NYC: $210 Million for 706 Community Projects," Participatory Budgeting Project, June 11, 2018, https:// www.participatorybudgeting.org/participatory-budgeting-in-nyc/.

28. Ginia Bellafante, "Participatory Budgeting Opens Up Voting to the Disenfranchised and Denied," *The New York Times*, April 17, 2015.

29. "Senators Representing Third or Minor Parties," United States Senate, https://www.senate.gov/senators/SenatorsRepresentingThirdorMinorParties .htm.

30. Richard Pearson, "Former Ala. Gov. George C. Wallace Dies," *The Washington Post*, September 14, 1998.

31. "Reelection Rates Over the Years," OpenSecrets.org, https://www .opensecrets.org/overview/reelect.php, accessed July 2019.

32. Ibid.

33. "Bold Gerrymander Reform Opens Up Florida Politics," Reclaim the American Dream (website), http://reclaimtheamericandream.org/success -gerrymander/, accessed July 2019.

34. Ibid.

35. Michael Wines, "Drive against Gerrymandering Finds New Life in Ballot Initiatives," *The New York Times*, July 23, 2018.

36. Jordan Misra, "Voter Turnout Rates among All Voting Age and Major Racial and Ethnic Groups Were Higher Than in 2014," The United States Census Bureau, April 23, 2019, https://www.census.gov/library/stories/2019/04/ behind-2018-united-states-midterm-election-turnout.html

37. Elections Canada, "Voter Registration Safeguards," https://www .elections.ca/content.aspx?section=vot&dir=bkg/safe&document=votReg& lang=e.

38. Tacey Rychter, "How Compulsory Voting Works: Australians Explain," *The New York Times,* October 22, 2018.

39. Kevin Morris and Peter Dunphy, "AVR Impact on State Voter Registration," Brennan Center for Justice, 2019, https://www.brennancenter.org/sites/ default/files/2019-08/Report_AVR_Impact_State_Voter_Registration.pdf.

Index

Index

Index

Index

Index

Index

Index

Index

Index

Acknowledgments

There are always many people for an author to thank at the time of publication of a book, but this time there are perhaps more people to thank, in more ways than usual.

I'd like to begin with my colleagues at the Martin Prosperity Institute. We set out on this journey together on July 1, 2013, with the inception of our project on the future of democratic capitalism, and wound it up on June 30, 2019, when MPI closed its doors. First, I want to give deep appreciation to my longtime thinking partner, Jennifer Riel, who has worked with me on thinking and writing projects for over a decade. I have profoundly valued our six years of intellectual sparring and her contribution to this book. Jamison Steeve served as Executive Director of MPI, and without his organization and leadership we would have ended up all over the map.

Stefanie Schram, Darren Karn, and Jacob Greenspon were our terrific researchers. I want to give special thanks to Darren, who has stayed on full-time to assist me right through to the publication of the book. And Jacob has continued to help with research as he completes his master's degree in public policy at the Harvard Kennedy School of Government, begun following the closing of MPI. Whoever hires him upon his graduation next year will be a lucky organization!

Jamison and I had terrific executive assistants, both of whom ended up getting deeply involved in the work of the institute. Quinn Davidson supported my MPI work, and Val Sladojevic-Sola supported Jamison's. Finally, our terrific designer, Michelle

Hopgood, made our work more readily understood and beautiful at the same time; she is responsible for all the graphics in the book.

Our work was aided by a fantastic group of MPI Fellows. Leading thinkers across a wide variety of relevant fields, they gave us ideas, critiqued our work, and provided unceasing encouragement. We couldn't have gotten to this point without Richard Florida, Adam Grant, Jonathan Haidt, Lauren Jones, Mariana Mazzucato, Nilofer Merchant, Mark Stabile, and Zeynep Ton.

We also received great guidance and support from the MPI board: Geoff Beattie (chair), Bill Downe, Arianna Huffington, Nina Mažar, Nandan Nilekani, Will Strange, and Tim Sullivan. I want to give a special thanks to publishing whiz Tim Sullivan, who gave me lots of patient and helpful feedback on multiple drafts of the book.

As the conclusions from our work started to take shape, we held roundtables in London, San Francisco, and New York that were enormously helpful in honing our thinking. I would like to thank all of the participants: Michael Birkin, Brett Bonthron, Tim Brown, Zachery First, Justin Fox, Bobby Ghosh, Lord Michael Hastings, Drew Houston, Adi Ignatius, Kenny Imafidon, Gareth Jones, Fred Leichter, Josh Macht, Geoff Mulgan, Sally Osberg, Steve Pearlstein, Eric Ries, Susan Schuman, Ron Shaich, and Sue Siddall.

I had the benefit of a pair of terrific thought partners across the course of the whole project: Peter Kadas and David Samuel. Previously, they were members of my Rotman Dean's Advisory Committee, and they continued to support me and my work at MPI.

A number of friends and colleagues read drafts of the book and contributed to its final form: Ellie Avishai, George Butterfield, Martha Butterfield, Brendan Calder, Stuart Crainer, Des Dearlove, Josie Fung, and Dani Rodrik.

In addition, I want to give a special thank you to the late Paul Volcker. Paul was always a great supporter of my work and a tough

Acknowledgments

but helpful critic. I sent him a draft manuscript in April 2019 and met with him at his Manhattan condo in May. He liked it but had many suggestions. I sent him a next iteration in July and we had a phone call in August—more suggestions. I sent him the third and last draft of the book in September and October 1, 2019, and his wife Anke Dening sent me an email with the endorsement that is on the cover. I hadn't even asked and thought at the time that it was pretty early. But I think that Paul perhaps had an inkling that his last days were not far away—and he was right, as he passed away on December 8, 2019. I will always treasure my discussions with that great man and am pleased to have his final endorsement.

This is my seventh book with Harvard Business Review Press, and I have a wonderful team there. Jeff Kehoe has been the acquiring editor for all seven of my books. Editor in chief Adi Ignatius is always a wonderful supporter of my work—whether it's a book like this or one of my many HBR articles. For this book, my longtime HBR article editor, David Champion, came onboard as the principal editor and made a significant and wonderful contribution to the final product. In addition, the team of Sally Ashworth, Julie Devoll, Stefani Finks, Erika Heilman, Felicia Sinusas, and Anne Starr were terrific as always.

For this book, I worked for the first time with the publicity team of Barbara Henricks and Jessica Krakoski, of Cave Henricks Communications, and it was a pleasure.

Last but not least, I want to thank my wife, Marie-Louise Skafte. Not only has she been helpful and supportive during the entire journey of MPI and the development of this book, but by introducing me to Joe's Stone Crab, she provided the perfect opening story for chapter 6. And thanks also for the support of our mutual friends here in Florida, Rachel-Ramona and Raymond.

Roger Martin
Fort Lauderdale, Florida

About the Author

ROGER L. MARTIN was named the world's number one management thinker in 2017 by Thinkers50, a biannual ranking of the most influential global business thinkers. He serves as a trusted strategy adviser to the CEOs of companies worldwide, including Procter & Gamble, LEGO, and Ford.

Martin is a Professor of Strategic Management, Emeritus, at the University of Toronto's Rotman School of Management, where he served as dean from 1998 to 2013. In 2013 he was named global Dean of the Year by the leading business-school website, Poets & Quants.

Martin is the author of eleven books, including *Creating Great Choices*, written with Jennifer Riel; *Getting Beyond Better*, written with Sally Osberg; and *Playing to Win*, written with A. G. Lafley, which won the Thinkers50 Best Book Award for 2013. In addition, he has written twenty-eight articles for *Harvard Business Review*.

Martin received his AB from Harvard College, with a concentration in economics, in 1979 and his MBA from Harvard Business School in 1981. He lives in South Florida with his wife, Marie-Louise Skafte.